POP CULTURE'S WAR

ON THE

AMERICAN FAMILY

BERNARD BERGERON BROUSSARD

pornography

raunchy radio

trash TV

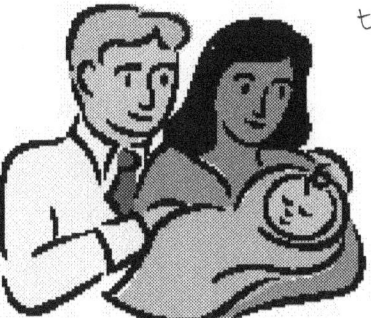

violence

sex-saturated
TV & movies

Vile, vulgar music

Agape
G · O · L · D
Gospel of Life Disciples

First published by AuthorHouse 04/30/05

ISBN: 1-4208-1947-X (sc)

Library of Congress Control Number: 2004195117

Printed in the United States of America
Bloomington, Indiana

This book is printed on acid-free paper.

authorHOUSE™

1663 Liberty Drive, Suite 200
Bloomington, Indiana 47403
(800) 839-8640
www.AuthorHouse.com

DEDICATION

For our lovely great-granddaughters —
Elizabeth Clare Parker and Brianna Parker Meche. We
pray that you will always strive to build a better world, a
world filled with Agape (love).
But remember: Your strength is in the Lord.
Bless you both.

Bernard & Rose Broussard
Your Great-Grandparents

TABLE OF CONTENTS

INTRODUCTION

Some will label me an undue alarmist, like the paranoid anti-Communists who used to see little "red" men behind every bush. But let's look at some hard (and very unpleasant) facts circa 2005. In 1970, there were over 300,000 drug arrests in our country, according to the Federal Bureau of Investigation. That number mushroomed to over 1.5 million at the turn of the century, much of it related to street crime generally, the decay of our cities, and the rising incidence of homeless persons.

Sexual promiscuity (I know, an unsavory word for those who refuse to label any human act as immoral) has assumed massive proportions. The proportion of births to teenagers in 1940 aged 15 to 19, for example, that occurred out of wedlock was 13.5 percent. By 1984, that number had shot up to 75.9 percent (as reported by the National Center for Health Statistics). The majority of marriages end in divorce, with devastating consequences for our nation's youth. When I was a teenager back in World War II, there were at most a handful of divorced couples in the town where I grew up. Now, there are a half dozen on the street where my wife and I live. Each class at Hanson Memorial (the Catholic high school I attended) has at least one, if not more, boys or girls whose parents are separated, divorced, or remarried. The term "single parent" has been firmly enshrined in our national lexicon.

Back then, when I was young, a girl who became pregnant was shipped off to another state, there to have and put out for adoption her child. Now, single mothers are attending high school in droves, and the spectacle of a very-much-pregnant girl walking up the aisle to be married no longer generates even an eyebrow lift from those attending. This is not to even mention the growing number of so-called same-sex unions, often participated in by practicing Catholics.

What we have is a dumbing down of America, a fact well documented by many, especially the late Steve Allen (Dumbth: The Lost Art of Thinking, and 101 Ways to Reason Better and Improve Your Mind), illustrates the fact that our nation's people are, pardon the expression, getting dumber.

Allen (Vulgarians at the Gate) also tells us, in a sense, to wake up and smell the coffee if we are blind to the social chaos now characteristic of American society and the junk yard aspects of much of American entertainment.

We all love our great nation. We boast at being the leader of the civilized world. And yet, the United States leads the world in the percentage of children born out of wedlock. Millions of abortions are performed every year, and most of our leading Catholic politicians continue bleating about "a woman's right to choose," in direct and public defiance to the church's express condemnation of the mindless holocaust of babies in the wombs of their mothers. In my own lifetime I have suffered through the assassinations of some of the best sons our nation has produced, from President John F. Kennedy to Martin Luther King, Jr., to Senator Robert Francis Kennedy. We have seen Malcolm X gunned down, President Reagan shot, and an attempt made on the life of President Gerald Ford.

Divorce has ripped asunder the American family, and the effect on our youth has been quite destructive. The U.S. leads the world in broken homes, two-fifths of our children no longer with their fathers. Over 15 million children without fathers. A recent report indicated an astonishing 42 percent of children from broken homes have not seen their fathers for over a year.

The point of all this shameful (sinful) behavior is that there is a direct connection between such awful realities on one hand and the constant exposure to television on the other. TV rules supreme, having more influence on our youth than our schools, churches, government, books, or newspapers. Not even parents can compete with the "boob tube"!

At one time, the TV exercised great social responsibility, exposing the brazen liars in the tobacco industry about the harmful effects of their product. Now the guys in suits have completely flip-flopped. They are mired in a serious state of denial. Now they seem deliberately set on a course to plunge our culture into a state of ugly depravity. The result in recent years is a moral numbing, a blind insensitivity to the awareness of evil. Marching in lock-step with our fellow citizens, we Catholics seem not to even care a whit about serious questions of right an wrong.

Oh, yes, we still become morally outraged at acts of terrorism and mindless shooting rampages, but the lesser atrocious offenses sneak right past our radar screens. We sit in a state of dulled tolerance while our kids are learning how to kill and maim with mindless and violent video games. We don't even bother to listen to the loathsome and woman-hating music of their rap and gangsta-rap music. We don't monitor (and most of the time actually join them) what our youth are viewing on TV (much of it on mainline), perhaps giggling self-consciously at the gutter-language, blatant sexuality, humping, and violence seen on practically every program.

The outrages on TV are too numerous to mention, nor do I intend to afford them free publicity here. A few examples will suffice, and for those who might be offended even by mentioning them in passing, you're free to skip forward to the next section.

We have lingerie-clad women offering sex advice from bed — Britney Spears cavorting on NBC in an outfit more suited for the French Quarter in New Orleans — women being trashed by "shock jocks" — sexual perambulations on daytime soaps — vulgarity on practically every show. Enough!

The worst offenders by the way are on prime time, from the killings and rantings of the Sopranos to the humpings on "Sex and the City," and the crude vulgarities of "Friends" and "Just Shoot Me."

Even in prison, those who have been convicted of offenses involving children are treated like someone inflicted with a deadly virus by their fellow inmates. And yet, on TV program after program, these vile sitcoms are spending their last ounce of energy trying to lure our youth into a world and culture of sexual irresponsibility and permissiveness. Truly, the devil never sleeps.

Poll after poll has shown that the American people believe that movies and TV have become too vulgar. Parents find themselves squirming (and hopefully blushing) when they view these TV programs and movies with their children.

But will the movie moguls and TV executives police their own products? Perish the thought. Said one executive: "The ratings will not affect anything we do, for one second. The whole point is to inform parents about what's on our schedule, not to edit what we put on the air." In other words, unless we rise up, unite, and do something about it, matters will only get worse.

Someone has said that today's culture has become one massive occasion of sin. We are literally saturation-bombed around the clock with ungarnished messages from the movies, television, radio, music, and every other means of communi-cation. The talking heads, the sitcoms, the soaps, the movies, the rap music, all shout out at us: "Hey, it's cool to be a libertine, to abort your child, to bed hop, to dump your marriage partner, to defend yourself with violence, to abandon your family, to dress immodestly, to use vile language, to do — your thing."

Our youth are the ones who suffer the most — worst of all because they have no idea of the dangerous mine field upon which they trod, like Dorothy walking into the field of poppies in The Wizard of Oz. Consequently, we have a young boy blithesomely singing along with the boom box on his shoulder as he strolls down the street, with a tune advocating the rape and violent abuse of women, or some other form of loathsome violence he has seen on "Dawson's Creek," "South Park," or even the "milder" stuff on "The Simpsons." Or perhaps he's just viewed the latest a-- kickin' karate movie or some of the slick, seductive images on MTV, or been influenced by the latest shock-jock cruelties.

A famous psychologist wrote a bestselling book a few years ago entitled, Whatever Happened to Sin? Well, it's still much with us, but now we realize that it's not just personal but social. It is all around us. On TV. In the movies. Video games. No longer is it in the margins. It comes into our homes every day. Our youth are awash in it, especially from TV, the most pervasive medium in history.

The soap operas and sitcoms are almost exclusively sleaze. The music is suggestive and debasing. The video games brainwash our children and inure them to the horror of violence.

I suppose by now you're clucking your tongue, sure that I'm one of those fools who comes along in each generation decrying the moral turpitude of our youth, criticizing its music and values, proclaiming to the heavens that "our young people are going to hell in a hand basket!"

I ask you to bear with me. Read on. Pray and reflect on some of the perils we, especially our youth, face. Learn more about where the drugs and vile music come from, and what kind of a sex-drug-violent culture it has generated.

Before we move on, here is one snippet from a review of Something about Mary, a revolting movie if ever there was one: "It was like a permission slip for movie makers everywhere to share their sickest, smelliest, suckiest toilet humor with the rest of the class." Another example? How about Austin Powers: The Spy Who Shagged Me, wherein the title character "sips a diarrhea daiquiri" and has "gerbils appears to pop out his butt."

Labeling? Self-policing? As said earlier, forget it. But what about parents? Surely they must see the danger. If they had been caring and intelligent enough, would we be slowly settling into a quicksand of muck and sleaze in 2005? And even when children do have concerned parents, can they possibly super-vise every minute of their children's watching or listening to audio or video material?

And then we have the millions of American children who spend long afternoons and nights at their friends' homes where they might be exposed to who knows what.

Then what are we to do, hang our heads and admit defeat? The last thing we must do is despair. There is a way out of this crisis. We who love God and cherish the teachings of our Catholic faith must believe that with our whole mind, heart, and soul. I hope in this little book to clearly identify the problems we and our children face, to identify the offenders, and to present a solution for us to consider. I do this prayerfully, asking our Lord's help in this vital endeavor.

—Bernard Bergeron Broussard

PART ONE

—

THE MAKING OF THE DRUGS-SEX-VIOLENCE CULTURE

Illegal drugs. Promiscuous sex. Moral decay. Defiance of lawful authority. Vile music. Devil worship. Girls being sold into lives of prostitution. If you shrugged your shoulders upon reading this litany of woes, sighed deeply and whispered, "So, true, but there's nothing new under the sun," you're right. These kinds of things have been going on since our First Parents were ejected from the Garden of Eden. But now, circa 2005, they are proliferating at any alarming rate. And in addition to these all-too-familiar human sins, we must regrettably add some we never had (on a widespread scale) to deal with before in Christian civilization for now children are killing each other, kids are killing their parents, parents are murdering their youth, and young people are committing suicide at the highest rate ever. We believe that much of it is deliberate and is a direct result of what some have called "America's Opium War Against Its Own Children." (Lyndon LaRouche)

We believe the wave of "cultural depravity" sweeping America has its roots in hard acid rock and "gangsta" music, the ever-spreading drug scene, the vile movies and TV programs coming forth from the media, the violent Nintendo and video games being produced by huge multi-billion dollar industries, the proliferating divorce rate, and the breakdown of the American family.

The "new violence" is a national security issue. The video and film industries continue to spawn new behavioral, emotional and physical problems, and increasing numbers of children — some younger than age one — are being fed steady diets of psychiatric drugs, according to the Journal of the American Medical Association (JAMA).

The evidence of this tragedy is all around us. In March 2000, Sabrina Steger, a pediatric nurse, testified on video games and violence before the U.S. Senate Committee on Commerce, Science and Transportation. But she is more than just a pediatric nurse; she is the mother of Kayce Steger, one of the three students killed at Heath High School in Paducah, Kentucky, on December 1, 1997, by 14-year-old Michael Corneal. She is also a plaintiff in a lawsuit against the makers, designers, and distributors of the killer video games to which young Corneal was addicted.

Said Steger: "I am the person you do not want to be. I live a parent's worst nightmare — eight shots fired, eight children hit in the upper chest, neck or head. Kayce, Jessica and Nicole died that day — we believe the Heath shooter was influenced by the movies he watched, the video games he played, and the Internet sites he used."

Corneal fired with deadly accuracy. Eight shots. Eight students wounded. And yet, Corneal had only been out once taking some kind of target practice. Even police officers were astounded that a mere 14-year-old boy with virtually no training in firing a weapon could be 100 percent accurate.

Where did Corneal acquire this deadly skill? It had to be from the use of Nintendo-style games, especially Pokemon.

What part, if any, have prescription drugs played in the Littleton-style shooting incidents we have been experiencing lately? Well, we do know that T.J. Salomon, the 15-year-old from Conyers, Georgia, who shot six classmates in May 1999, was on Ritalin. We know that Eric Harris, the 15-year-old from Springfield, Oregon, who killed his parents and two schoolmates and wounded twenty other students in May 1998, had been prescribed the antidepressant Prozac, one of the most widely prescribed drugs.

Of the over 6,000,000 kids under age 18 in America who have been prescribed Ritalin, Luvox, Prozac, Paxil, and other antidepressants and psychiatric drugs for emotional and behavioral problems, large numbers have committed violent acts, even killings. And many more are what some have called "walking time bombs." (Michelle Steinberg, The New Federalist)

Other instances: On March 6, 2000, 16-year-old Jarred Viktor stabbed his grandmother 61 times. He was on Paxil. In Kansas, 13-year-old Mat Miller, on the antidepressant Zoloft, took his own life.

Still, with evidence mounting of the possible harmful effects caused by these drugs, thousands of infants, toddlers, and preschool children are being zombified with psychiatric drugs — produced for adults — before they even learn to talk, let alone read.

The most targeted population for these drugs are African-American children and those diagnosed with Attention Deficit Hyperactivity Disorder (ADHD). They are prescribed the stimulant Ritalin (methylphenidate) at younger and younger ages, with the number of prescriptions in two study groups having increased more than 300% during 1991-95. Prozac is also being abused. A 1994 report compiled by the Food and Drug Administration reported some 3,000 prescriptions for fluoxetine hydrochloride (the generic name for Prozac) had been written for children younger than one year of age. These findings were revealed by a team of doctors from the

University of Maryland and the Center for Health Research, Kaiser Permanente, in Portland, Oregon, at the annual meeting of the American Psychiatric Association in Washington, D.C.

After analyzing ambulatory care prescription records covering over four years from Medicaid programs and HMOs (Health Maintenance Organizations), researchers published results that were enough to send a shock wave through the nation. All of the findings showed a strong increase of psychotropic medication prescriptions for preschoolers. Methylphenidate use had increased at all three sites used in the tests participating in the 1991-1995 study, and this included records covering over 200,000 patients.

Poor children were the most affected. The results from 1988 showed the following: "Pediatric researchers noted that 57% of 223 Michigan Medicaid enrollees aged younger than four years with a diagnosis of ADHD received at least one psychotropic medication to treat this condition. Methylphenidate led the list of medications administered." The label of every bottle of Ritalin has the following warning printed on it:

WARNING: Ritalin should not be used in children under six years, since safety and efficacy in this age group has not been established.

A second warning says:

PRECAUTIONS: Long-term effects of Ritalin in children have not been well established.

Ritalin has been responsible for a number of children who have taken normal doses becoming violent, and the drug is one of the ten most abused in the nation.

HMOs are the U.S. version of Nazi drug dispensaries. Too strong a condemnation? Think so — then consider the following facts. A United Nations' report on international drug trends, issued in 1999, indicated that 85 to 90% of the MPD (methylphenidate, or Ritalin) produced in the world is consumed in the United States.

4

Health insurance plans, especially HMOs, will not finance therapy or counselling for children, so they give them dope. Lots of it. Especially if they have ADHD.

This runaway prescribing of antidepressants for children (over 3,000,000 in 1999) is due, in the main, from pressure from managed health care. As mentioned previously, they refuse to pay for long-term treatment. Writes Rab Waters in Family Therapy Networker: "This prescribing of drugs as a substitute for therapy means that children are being given unproven treatments more haphazardly and with fewer practical and legal protections than adults who volunteer to be paid subjects in the clinical trials of new drugs." Waters warns that these drugs could have severe physical and psychological side effects.

Some of the doctors involved have expressed reservations about Ritalin, et al, but frankly assert their doubts that the children's families can get around managed health care barriers to therapy. The doctors admit that the health plan may refuse to pay for long months of treatment. The situation is compounded for children of low income families.

Dr. Joseph Woolson, medical director of the children's psychiatric drug unit at Yale-New Haven Hospital, has said that the prescribing of psychoactive drugs to children is skyrocketing. "Every single day we have at least one case where the managed health care reviewer says to us that if we don't start the child on medications within 24 hours after admission, they will not fund another day of hospital."

There is intense economic incentive to let a child take Ritalin. The incentive? Extra money for the physicians. A 1996 report reveals the fact that Social Security once considered ADHD a "disability." So the economic incentive is incredible. A disabled child can receive up to $470 a month in a low income family, especially one on welfare. Not much money, but consider such states as Mississippi and Texas, where poor children and families receive about $201 for a family of three, slightly over $2,400 per year.

Once there is an ADHD diagnosis, there must be a "treatment" or child and family won't qualify for further payment eligibility including Medicaid or Medicare. And the only treatments paid for by managed care, including Medicaid, is psychiatric drugs. Once on Ritalin, unless there is intervention, the poor child will be on the drug for life.

Can it be more clear? Our children are being subjected to drug violence.

But that's only part of the horror story. Our children, even under age five, are being caught up in an emotional hell. The drugs are part of the horror. A big part! Then there is the violence spewing from the video and film industries. Even babies are being given psychiatric drugs in ever-increasing numbers. Prozac, stimulants, or combinations thereof, adult medicines, are being prescribed for mere babies.

Many believe Ritalin has its origins in the Nazi eugenics movement of the 1930s. Avril Harriman of the U.S., for instance, was a big booster of the Nazi eugenic policy.

Then there was Aldous Huxley and his Brave New World in 1932, followed by the first prefrontal brain lobotomy for mental illness in 1935, and in 1937, the first use of stimulants in the treatment of so-called "hyperactivity" in children. Part of the eugenics movement was identification, isolation, and eventual elimination of people who were afflicted with mental illness or who might have a genetic background that could end up in a mental disorder.

Huxley envisioned a futuristic "world government" that sought to create "perfect, genetically engineered human beings." Since control must start with the fetus, all babies in Huxley's fantasy would be grown in test tubes and developed into different levels of intelligence and capabilities. The upper class — the intellectuals, the ruling class — would be composed of the "Alphas," and those fetuses would get sufficient nutrients and oxygen for them to develop to their maximum. Next would be the "Betas," lower than the Alphas, but still among the rulers. All work in society would be done by the genetically engineered lower classes: "Deltas," "Gammas," and "Epsilons."

The emotions of all these classes would have to be controlled, so Huxley introduces a drug of pacification called "soma," which is given to keep everyone happy, quiet, and a stranger to all trouble-making or disturbance of any kind. Ritalin is fast becoming our latter-day soma. After years of taking the drug, "There is little improvement in academic achievement or social skills," says the National Institute of Health (NIH). While aggression may be tempered, children on Ritalin "still manifest a higher level of some behavior problems than normal children."

The "cutting down on aggressiveness" is very problematic. T.J. Salomon, a Georgia boy, went to school and shot six classmates in May 1999. He was on Ritalin. Other shootings and mass killings have also involved children on the drug.

The New Violence

We desperately need research on how to cure our children of the mental illnesses being caused by the new violence. What is this new violence? It is Nintendo-type games that seek to transform young children and adolescents, as well as law enforcement personnel, into "Samurai-style," programmed killers. We are speaking here of the new violence along the Littleton-Columbine style in which Nintendo-style games and related methods and means are crucial, distinguishing features that appear in these crimes. This includes the use of related methods and objectives in the training and deployment of law enforcement agents or analogous instances.

To further investigate and analyze this new violence, we utilize the utopian program conceptualized by H.G. Wells' The Open Conspiracy and Huxley's utopian "New Age" models, as well as those of Bertrand Russell's in the movie Clockwork Orange, as points of reference. What is specifically new is the adaptation of the mythos of the Samurai warriors and related "martial arts" mythology, combined with such madness as "Dungeons and Dragons," and Tolkein's Lord of the Rings. Also, we will look at the mad-killer pornography of cinematic cartoons and Nintendo-style games. The use of this method and its derivatives for the purpose of programmed conditioning of military personnel, law enforcement teams, and for indoctrinating children into a programmed impulse response for terrorist forms of violence is adequately understood only when such Nintendo-game conditioning is situated within the utopian doctrine of Bertrand Russell's program to deal with so-called population control, which he sought to utilize in order to bring about the oligarchical utopian ends visualized by H.G. Wells.

To more thoroughly understand today's drug-sex-violence syndrome, let's look at the origins of what is called "the aquarian conspiracy."

A book entitled The Aquarian Conspiracy appeared in 1980, and the author, Marilyn Ferguson, puts the work forward as a manifesto of the counterculture. She defines this so-called counterculture as the conscious embracing of irrationality, from rock and drugs to biofeedback, meditation, "consciousness-raising," yoga, group therapy, psychodrama, and mountain climbing. This aquarian conspiracy declares that it is now time for the 15 million Americans involved in the counterculture to join in bringing about "a radical change in the United States."

Ferguson writes: "While outlining a not-yet titled book about emerging social alternatives, I thought again about the peculiar form of this movement, its atypical leadership, the patient intensity of its adherents, their unlikely successes." These dope peddlers had a precedent for the counterculture they imposed upon the US: the bogus cult ceremonies of the decaying Roman Empire.

The acts or gestures that accompany incantations constitute the rite [of Isis]. In these dances, the beating of drums and the rhythm of music and repetitive movements were helped by hallucinatory substances like hashish or mescal; these were consumed as adjuvants to create the trance and the visitation of the god. The drugs were sacred, and their knowledge was limited to the initiated.

Possibly because they have the illusion of satisfied desires, and allowed the innermost feelings to escape, these rites acquired during the execution of a frenzied character that is conspicuous in certain spells: "Retreat! Re is piercing the head, slashing thy face, dividing thy head, crushing it in his hands; thy bones are shattered, thy limbs are cut to pieces."

The counterculture imposed on the youth of America in the chaotic 1960s is not merely analogous to the ancient cult of the Isis. It is a literal resurrection of the cult— down to the Isis cross as the counterculture's most frequently used symbol.

Aldous Huxley, mentioned prominently, was the high priest of Britain's unrelenting Opium Wars. He had a lifelong collaboration in historian Arnold Toynbee, a veteran of the Wars and head of the Research Division of British Intelligence in World War II, serving under Prime Minister Winston Churchill.

Toynbee, in his 20-volume history of Western Civilization, expounded a theory that its most prevailing feature has always been the rise and decline of grand imperial dynasties. Rome fell, as did the reign of the Roman pharaohs, and now his own British empire strode the globe like a colossus. It, too, would decline and fade eventually into the dust bin of history — unless, he urged, that the British Roundtable would devote itself to the recruitment and training of an ever-expanding priesthood devoted to the principles of imperial rule.

Toynbee was an initiate in the Dionysian cult known as the "Children of the Sun," comprised of the children of England's Roundtable elite. His fellow members included T.S. Eliot, W.H. Auden, Sir Oswald Mosley, and D.H. Lawrence, who was Huxley's homosexual lover. Some years later, Huxley led the fight to overcome the move to ban Lawrences' Lady Chatterly's Lover from coming into the U.S. on the grounds that it was "pornographic." Huxley lamented: "This novel is a misunderstood work of art."

The spiritual grandfather of the Aquarian Conspiracy was the novelist H.G. Wells, the head of the British Foreign Intelligence during World War I, who sought the open conspiracy, Blue Prints for a World Revolution. It was a scheme for a new world order, a movement of intelligentsia (wealthy intelligencia) that would ultimately produce a "one-world brain." This one-world brain would function as "a police of the mind."

Much of Wells's popular writings (Time Machine, The Island of Doctor Moreau) and those of his proteges Aldous Huxley (Brave New World) and George Orwell (1984 and Animal Farm) were written as "mass appeal" organizing documents on behalf of one-world order. Only in the United States are these "science fiction classics" taught in grade school as "attacks" against fascism.

Later, Huxley and Aleister Crowley, together with poet William Butler Yeats, formed the Isis-Urania Temple of Hermetic Students of the Golden Dawn. This Isis Cult was organized around the 1877 book Isis Unveiled by Madame Helina Blavatsky, in which the Russian occultist called for the British aristocracy to organize itself into an Isis priesthood.

Huxley came to the U.S. in 1937 and remained throughout World War II. He landed a job as a script writer for MGM in a Hollywood dominated by organized crime figures such as "Bugsy" Seigel, the West Coast boss of the Meyer Lansky syndicate.

In Southern California, Huxley founded a nest of Isis cults. They were eventually joined by Thomas Mann and his daughter Elizabeth Mann Borghese. Together they laid the foundations for the later LSD culture, by recruiting a core of "initiates" into the Isis cults that Huxley's mentors Burliver-Lytton, Blavatsky, and Crowley had constituted while stationed in India.

The watershed for mescaline was May, 1953, when Humphrey Osmond introduced it to Huxley in Hollywood. The trip made him ecstatic. "I was seeing what Adam had seen on the morning of his creation — the miracle moment by moment, of naked existence." He recorded his experiences in Doors of Perception and Heaven and Hell in 1954, and advocated its use in the article at the end of The Humanist Frame in 1961, as a means to higher human potentialities. He later came to believe that biochemical mysticism could be the key to his "philosophia perennis." He proclaimed that behind all the world religious there could be discerned and ultimate truth of which each religion was only a partial expression.

LSD

LSD, a synthetic chemical, has no pre-history, although for centuries there was a parasitic fungus called ergot which caused chaos whenever found in cultivated fields of rye. The aberrations and visual disturbances are called St. Anthony's Fire. One active substance of this fungus was lysergic acid, although this in itself is not hallucinogenic.

Dr. Albert Hoffman, working in the Sandoz laboratories overlooking the Rhine in Switzerland, first synthesized LSD in 1928. LSD-25 was the 25th variety he had developed. Researching a painkiller for migraine, he added a diethylamide to the lysergic acid to make lysergic acid diethylamide. He experienced his own acid trip and his notebooks quickly degenerate into absolute incoherence. This so-called "miracle drug" soon became a "nightmare drug."

Ironically, LSD was introduced through the Central Intelligence Agency's (CIA) investigation into the substances for possible military use. Experiments on more than eighty campuses, under various CIA code names, unintentionally popularized LSD. Thousands of graduate students served as guinea pigs, and soon they were synthesizing their own "acid."

The CIA operation was code named MK-Ultra, and strangely began in 1952, the year Aldous Huxley came to live in southern California. Huxley was given a supply of mescaline for his personal consumption in 1953. The next year he wrote The Doors of Perception , the first manifesto of the psychedelic drug cult, which claimed that hallucinogenic drugs "expanded consciousness."

In 1962, the Rand Corporation, following the lead of the Ford Foundation, began a four year experiment in LSD. Rand was the outgrowth of the Wartime Strategic Bombing Survey, a "cost analysis" study of the bombings of German population centers.

According to a 1952 Rand Abstract, W.H. McGlothlin conducted a preparatory study on "the Long-Lasting Effects of LSD on Certain Attitudes in Normals: An Experimental Proposal." The following year, McGlothlin conducted a year long experiment on 30 human guinea pigs, called "Short-term Effects of LSD on anxiety, attitudes and performance." The study concluded that "LSD <u>improved</u> emotional attitudes and resolved anxiety problems."

Let us remember that the CIA, solely responsible for these grotesque experiments in the first place, was and is a tool of those forces which control government. It is these forces who initiated the deadly MK-Ultra and similar such programs.

CIA Chief Allen Dulles developed the MK-Ultra project under the guidance of the fascist psychoanalyst Carl Jung. Yes, the same Carl Jung who has become guru to millions of misguided Catholics of our time. Carl Jung and Allen Dulles worked hand-in-hand with a very precise plan in mind: the creation of a counterculture; a new dark age!

One of the famous, or should we say infamous, groups, spawned by this whole evil witches' brew was the so-called "Church of the Awakening." A group sans doctrine but with a sacrament — a drug induced psychedelic experience — dispensed to all members once every three months. The Neo-American Church took an even more militant stand on the legality of using peyote as a sacrament.

Thus had begun the brainwashing of a whole generation of young people, many of whom occupy central positions in our very sick, God-starved society.

The CIA sponsored LSD experiments of the 1950s and 1960s began when Allen Dulles met Carl Jung at the Harvard University Tercentenary Conference in 1936. Jung was at the time president of the International Medical Society of Psychotherapy, headquartered in Zurich. Thus began a close collaboration between spymaster Dulles and Jung, whose occultist theories of racial memory were the psychiatric equivalent of Nazi ideology.

The charismatic influence of several men helped spread the new counterculture in the post World War II years. Besides

Dulles, Huxley and Jung, we must consider Dr. Timothy Leary, author Ken Kesey, Dr. Gregory Bateson, and Allan Watts.

Leary, who died in 1996, was the high priest, its messiah and martyr. The former Roman Catholic turned into a self-proclaimed "smart-aleck atheist," actually promoted LSD as a new "evolutionary religion." Said he, "The LSD kick is a spiritual ecstasy," — "the way to grove to the music of God's song." He encouraged people to, "Start your own religion," "Write your own Bible," "Write your own ten commandments."

It was all a kind of bizarre psychic-Darwinism where the tripper is the new man and LSD is the "sacrament which will put you in touch with the ancient two-million year-old wisdom inside you" freeing you "to go on to the next stage which is the evolutionary timelessness, the ancient reincarnation theory that we always carry inside."

Leary and Huxley put their heads together and "talked about how to study the use of the consciousness-expanding drugs" and they were in total agreement that they should not be limited by the pathological point of view. "We were not to interpret ecstasy as mania, or calm serenity as catatonia; we were not to diagnose Buddha as a detached schizoid; nor Christ as an exhibitionist masochist; nor the mystic experience as a model psychosis."

From these brainstorming sessions, Huxley and Leary decided upon a pilot study, in which the subjects would be treated like astronauts.

It was in 1960, when Leary went to Cuenavaca, that he first tried the magic mushrooms, which he later claimed "put many, if not everyone, within reach of a visionary state without having to suffer the mortifications of Blake and St. John. It permits one to know God."

So Huxley and Leary's new pilot project would consist of extensive experiments with a synthetic form of the "magic mushroom." First, they decided, it must be introduced to what they considered to be the cultural elite. This included members of the Beat Generation and other friends of Allen Ginsberg, as well as an assortment of artists, scholars, and screen moguls.

One of that "elite" group was Ken Kesey who, despite his meeting with the high priest of acid as "a crypt trip," turned millions of young people against the establishment with such radical novels as One Flew Over the Cuckoo's Nest.

Another influential elite was Herman Hesse, whose novel Steppenwolf was the bible for the first celebration of Leary's groups. Huxley said "the English are the original hippies," singing the praises of a pedigree of psychedelics coming down from Humphrey Osmond, Aldous Huxley, Alan Watts, R.D. Laing, and Paul McCartney.

In the early days, acid taking was by no means limited to the counterculture, though, for even such a well known celebrities as Cary Grant, Herman Kahn, and Henry Luce claimed to have tripped.

Leary and Huxley recruited a number of theologians to their project. Among them, Walter Clard, Professor Emeritus in the Psychology of Religion at Andover-Newton Theological School, who wrote extensively about the famous William James. Leary and Clark ran a session for Professor Houston Smith, Chairman of the MIT Philosophy Department. Smith then ran psilocybin sessions for MIT undergraduates and graduate students laboratory exercises for his seminars on mysticism.

Leary and Huxley collaborated to produce a manual for the drug culture taken from the Tibetan Book of the Dead, in which they claimed that LSD "liberated" the brain from structures of reason and morality because the drug prevented coherent thought and distorted perceptions.

According to Leary and Huxley, the drugged vision of the world as a kaleidoscope of weirdly pulsating images, is in fact "truth."

Aldous Huxley, it might be noted, was trained by Dr. Thomas Huxley, the man who helped Charles Darwin to fame. He was the grandfather of Aldous, and a close friend of atheist philosopher Bertrand Russell.

His most famous novel, Brave New World, written in 1927, is the prospectus for the counterculture developed by him, under the guidance of his mentors H.G. Wells and Bertrand Russell. The society which he describes was organized to reward its slaves with hedonistic delights provided by drugs and three-dimensional television, which included sensual stimulation as well. A slave state, in which the lower orders had been genetically engineered to an animal-like stupidity and placidity.

Huxley had an evil vision of utopia, and a widespread drug culture. He well understood that the counterculture which he helped to create would be spawning ground for satanism.

Meanwhile, Ken Kesey, in 1959, had been administered his first dose of LSD at Palo Alto VA hospital by the aforementioned Dr. Gregory Bateson.

Kesey completed his novel, One Flew Over the Cuckoo's Nest in 1962, popularizing the notion that society is a prison and the only truly "free" people are the insane.

Kesey later organized a circle of LSD initiates called "the Merry Pranksters," who toured the country disseminating LSD, building up local distribution connections, and establishing the pretext for a high volume of publicity on behalf of the still very small circle of counterculture devotees.

By 1967, the Kesey cult had hooked a sizeable number of acid trippers, with the main body of followers in the Haight-Asbury district of San Fransisco. Bateson and Kesey proceeded to set up a "free clinic," paralleling a project at the Tavistock Institute in London where mind-expanding drugs were routinely used in the treatment of patients. In 1967, Tavistock sponsored a conference on the "Dialectics of Liberation," chaired by Dr. R.D. Laing, another confirmed drug user. Among those attending were Angela Davis and Stokely Carmichael, two who would soon be playing prominent roles in fostering terrorism. Before 1967 had ended, the cult "Flower Children" of Height Asbury had been set loose to flood the nation with hashish and marijuana.

The "Lads from Liverpool" made their heralded debut in the U.S. in 1963, closely followed by the Rolling Stones, and the homicidal punk rock fanatics who rushed behind them were no more a spontaneous outpouring of alienated youth than was the acid culture they accompanied.

The social theory of rock was elaborated by musicologist Theodore Adorno, who came to the U.S. in 1939 to head the Princeton University Radio Research Project. Adorno writes:

> In an imaginary but psychologically emotion-laden domain, the listener who remembers a hit song will turn into the song's ideal subject, into the person for whom the song ideally speaks. At the same time, as one of many who identify with that fictitious subject, that musical, he will feel his isolation ease as he himself feels integrated into the community of "fans." In whistling such a song he bows to the ritual of socialization, although beyond this unarticulated subjective stirring of the moment his isolation continues unchanged.

> . . . The comparison with addiction is inescapable. Addicted conduct generally has a social component: it is one possible reaction to the atomization which, as sociologists have noticed, parallels the compression of a social network. Addiction to music on the part of a number of entertainment listeners would be a similar phenomenon.

The post World War II Hit Parade transformed the mass medium into an agency of subcultural programming. Radio networks were converted into round the clock recycling machines that repeated the top forty "hits." Thus does all so-called popular culture - movies, music, books, and fashion— all run on the same program of preselection. Today's mass culture operated like the opium trade: The supply determines the demand.

VIETNAM - AND THE ANTI-WAR MOVEMENT

Save for the unpopular Vietnam War, the Isis cult would have been contained to a fringe cult no bigger than the beatnik cult of the 1950s. The endless war in Asia prepared the soil wherein grew the moral despair that opened America's youth to the curse of drugs.

And where did the drugs that swamped the anti-war movement on America's college campuses come from? Nowhere else but America's organized crime infrastructure.

Unlike his predecessor, Dwight Eisenhower (who had decided not to become directly involved in the Vietnam struggle), Kennedy began to send some small contingents of American military to that embattled nation. Lyndon Johnson, who took office following Kennedy's assassination, lent his ear to the Anglophile Eastern Establishment, typified by top White House national security aide McGeorge Bundy and defense secretary Robert McNamara, who convinced the skeptical president to throw the full weight of America's military might into the fray. They persuaded Johnson that under the nuclear "balance of terror," or the regime of Mutual and Assured Destruction, the United States could afford neither a political solution to the ever-widening conflict, nor the commitment to a military victory.

This utter debacle eventually led to a major strategic withdrawal from Asia by the United States. Henry Kissinger spelled it all out in his "Guam Doctrine." This incredible blunder added up to the adoption of the failed "China Card" strategy for containing Soviet influence, leading to the demoralization of the American people over the war. Our sense of national pride and confidence in the future progress of the republic was dealt an almost fatal blow.

The mutual shadows of Lord Bertrand Russell and Aldous Huxley loom large here. Russell's passionate pacifism was always relative. He sought ultimately a one-world government on the imperial model, all designed to curb the nation-state and the persistent tendency toward republicanism and technological progress.

17

Both Huxley and Russell, for instance, cuddled up to Herr Hitler, opposing British and American warfare against the German tyrant. Russell in the 1950s advocated a preemptive nuclear strike against Russia. His celebrated "Ban the Bomb" movement was merely an anti-technology scheme which stood in opposition to the peace-through-economic development advocated by President Eisenhower's "Atoms For Peace" initiative.

Russell's "so-called" anti-war (and anti-American) movement of the Vietnam era, helped to revitalize the "New Left" using of the Social Democratic Party. New York banks provided several hundreds of thousand dollars to institute the Institute for Policy Studies (IPS), headed up by Marcus Raskin, a former member of Kennedy's National Security Council.

IPS eventually financed and directed the students for Democratic Society (SDS), the umbrella of the student anti-war movement, even through and beyond its splintering into a number of terrorist and Maoist gangs in the late 1960s. The Ford Foundation also provided seed money.

Among the lecturers and fellows of IPS we find such people as members of the Japanese Red Army, the Puerto Rican terrorist Armed Forces of Liberation and the Black Liberation Army. The U.S. anti-war movement and outlook was largely dominated by the direct political descendants of the British-dominated "socialist movement," fostered by the House of Morgan as for back as World War I.

The movement itself, however, at the grass roots, was filled with idealistic people who were disenchanted with the progress of the war in Vietnam. Swelling those ranks were very religious people, Catholic, Protestant, Jew, black and white, young and old, who simply believed that violence and war went against their deepest religious beliefs. Sadly, though, thousands of anti-war protestors, convinced by the followers of Russell to adopt a hedonistic life-style, had their sense of values and creative potential go up in a veritable cloud of hashish smoke.

Many years have passed since the Vietnam/Civil Rights era, and an entire generation of American youth has been submerged in a tidal wave of drugs. The very failure of our nation has been subverted, even to the topmost level of the government. The aquarian conspiracy dreamed of by Marilyn Ferguson is a success beyond her wildest imaginings.

Huxley founded the Esalen Institute in Big Sur, California, in 1962. It became a Mecca for hundreds of Americans to engage in T-Groups and Training Groups modeled on behavior group therapy, for Zen, Hindu, and Buddhist transcendental meditation, and "out of body" experiences through simulated and actual hallucinogenic drugs.

Esalen set out to bring together a wide variety of approaches to enhancement of the human potential, including encounter groups and gestalt awareness training at schools, hospitals, and churches. Since its inception, tens of thousands of Americans have passed through Esalen, while millions have taken part in its multiple programs.

The next step of the aquarian conspiracy against the U.S. was a 1974 report that provided the basis of Ferguson's work: "Changing Images of Man," Contract Number URH (489)-2150, Policy Research Report No. 414.74, prepared by the Stanford Research Institute Center for the Study of Social Policy.

The 319-page report was prepared by a group of 14 and supervised by a panel of 23 controllers, including anthropologist Margaret Mead, psychologist B.F. Skinner, Ervin Laszlo of the U.N. and Sir Geoffrey Vickers of British Intelligence.

The stated aim of the report was to change the image of mankind from that of industrial progress to one of "spiritualism." The image of industrial and technological man, the report asserts, is "obsolete and must be discarded."

The images found most dangerous and obsolete by the report are science, technology, and economics, even though all have "made possible really significant strides toward achieving such basic human goals as physical safety, material comfort, and better health." The report asserts that these gains have ushered in problems of being too successful — problems that seem insoluble within the set of societal value - premises that led to their emergence — Our highly developed system of technology leads to higher vulnerability and breakdowns. Indeed the range and interconnected impact of societal problems that are now emerging pose a serious threat to our civilization.. If our projections of the future prove correct, we can expect the association problems of the trend to become more serious, more universal and to occur more rapidly.

So, the images of man that dominated the past two centuries are found to be inadequate for post-industrial era.

Britain's creation of the counterculture to open the market for dope has come a long way.

PART TWO

—

THE BRAINWASHING: MOVIES, VIDEO GAMES, ROCK-ACID MUSIC, NEW AGE NUTTINESS

Let us begin by trying to just very briefly get into the minds of Eric Harris and Dyland Klebold, the two young men responsible for the terrible shootings at Columbine High School, Littleton, Colorado, in July of 1998.

Littleton, Colorado: a wealthy suburb with one of the most highly regarded school systems in America. But there had been curious happenings there long before the atrocious shootings. A teacher was fired because he had a history seminar in which he utilized movies as an educational tool. But some of the movies included the highly controversial Natural Born Killers, Pulp Fiction and Basketball Diaries. A number of parents were incensed upon learning about these particular movies being used as teaching aids in the classroom, and the teacher in question was dismissed for, in essence, showing pornographic material to teens. Well, it wasn't long before the fired teacher became a lightning rod for celebrities and civil activists, all of whom began bleating about First Amendment rights being trampled on by the forces of reactionism in Littleton. Klebold and Harris were, no doubt, ardent admirers of the embattled teacher, now the champion of every ultra liberal in sight.

A huge battle followed in the wake of the firing. Court cases ensued. But Columbine was no stranger to notoriety. The school had been featured prominently in 1990 on "20-20" because it had pioneered a radical course called "Death Education," which was a mandatory course in the school. In the course, children were subjected to "experiencing death." Kids had to visit morgues, where they viewed corpses and even sat in on autopsies. The teacher argued, "Well, death is part of everyone's experience, and therefore, it's good for people to learn to come to grips with it." In reality, it was all part of a process of desensitization, which means that suddenly issues that are fundamental philosophical and moral issues cease to exist, and everything is one succession of sensory experiences that all lead a person to abandon that which is essentially human in one's self.

Columbine, too, was on the cutting edge of New Age learning. Many (one out of three) of the students were on Prozac or Ritalin, prescribed for them by a high school guidance counselor — sanctioned drug use, mandated by the school system.

Harris and Klebold. This was the school environment in which their impressionable young minds gave way to evil — death education, New Age, Ritalin, their favorite movies: Basketball Diaries and Natural Born Killers, along with video games "Marine Doom" and "Pokemon."

As early as 1972, the Surgeon General's report warned about a link between media violence and violent behavior in children. The American Medical Association years ago said that media violence was our nation's number one health care emergency. No matter the media's denial and obfuscation of these facts, they remain unrefuted. Harris, Klebold, and Columbine are proof positive of the assertions made in both reports.

Let's examine even closer some of the movies and video games which so influenced the killers at Littleton, Colorado, as well as several other high schools throughout the United States.

Natural Born Killers played a key role in the Columbine massacre. Following is some of the script:

Rock music. Laughter. Gunshots.

"Greasy, f---- pig! ---/ You're less than a man. Are you clean? Or are you sloppy and wet? You stupid b------!"

Crash. Ghoulish laughter. Screams.

Now, in the movie, the mother is burned in the bed. The father is stabbed and drowned.

Screams. Rock music.

"They're hot. They're hot!"

The killers are celebrated by teenagers around the world, interviewed on TV talk shows because they murdered their parents.

Rock music. Yelling. Gunshots. Screams.

"You ain't seen nothin' yet!"

Laughter.

"Sh--, man. I'm a natural born killer."

Now, from the Basketball Diaries:

"It was death for the first time. His face was thin and wrinkled, almost ape-like. His hair, just gray patches on his scalp. He looked 60 years old, and he was 16."

Rock song!

"He was 12 years old, fell from the roof on East Two-Nine. Kathy was 11 when she pulled the plug; 20 cigarettes and a bottle of wine; Bobby ------ looked like 55 when he died. He was a friend of mine."

"Might as well mainline. I'm scared of needles. But I gave in."

Loud music.

The role of drugs, of course, is a crucial element in all this.

"It was a long heat wave through my body. Any ache or pain or sadness or guilt feeling was completely flushed out."

Woman's voice: "You just go right down to this corner and you make a left. It's right there. What are you doing? Let go. Let go. Let go of that!!"

Loud noises, scuffle, SCREAMS.

Male voice: "What are you doin'?"

Screams.

"GO!"

Traffic noise.

Loud rock music.

Boy goes into the classroom and shoots the students and the teacher.

Sound familiar? It should because it is exactly the way Harris and Klebold did the shooting at Littleton.

Heavy metal rock; percussion sounds. Weird voices. Screams. Roars.

Male voice: "I love the ritual."

Female voice: "Oh, man, if you can -----."

Drug dealers are shown.

More rock music.

"F--- em."

"What's your problem, man?"

"You sold my girlfriend some sh-- the other day. You almost killed her. What'd you put in that, rat poison?"

"Hey, man, I need you to give me some money. Okay?"

"I want the money. I want the money in the house. Where's the f------ money?"

Aaaggghhhh. Screams.

"No!"

Rock music, heavy beat.

The Satanic Roots of Rock Music —
and a Look at Today's Popular Music

Since the 1960s, rock music has served as a vehicle for the transmission of the satanic, drug-oriented counterculture.

1969 was the year of the Dionysian Festival; it was the culmination of the decade of Cultural Revolution during which the worship of Dionysus became this nation's established religion.

Strong statements. But oh so true! And none of all this came about by accident. Rather, it represents a deliberate policy, conjured up by those who promote this music and sponsor its performers. Money, no doubt, is part of the package. But above all, rock, acid, and such forms of so-called music is a vicious ideological tool used by unscrupulous persons. For over a generation these evil minds have been determined to brainwash the youth of our nation.

The drug scene, of course, is not new. Jazz and blues performers and many members of bands in the 1930s and 1940s had problems with drugs and alcohol. Difference was, come the 1960s and the evil genius of Aldous Huxley and Tim Leary, drugs were no longer thought of as a problem. Instead, the "drugged vision" became the paradigm for popular culture as a whole. Drug addicts like the Rolling Stones and the Beatles became media darlings and were lionized by naive youth around the world.

Even after the Stones were arrested for drug possession, the prestigious London Times vigorously defended them. The Stones, in turn, responded with a verbal attack on society's "out dated laws and mores," asserting their unwavering determination to "question some fundamental injustices," such as "the persecution of homosexuals and the prohibition of abortion and drug consumption." Finally, they lashed out at organized religion, as John Lennon later was to do, many times, stating, "Our friends ask themselves whether it is intelligent to accept religion almost blindly on the one hand and on the other hand totally deny things like UFO's, which seem to us closer to reality."

The songs, the music, the rock stars, all made drug consumption into a mass phenomenon among gullible youngsters. Virtually every rock star of that era took illegal drugs, glorified drug consumption in their songs, and sooner or later died themselves from bad trips and overdoses. The Lads from Liverpool paid homage to the psychedelic wave with "Yellow Submarine" and "Lucy in the Sky with Diamonds." The Rolling Stones were more explicit with "Sister Morphine," "Cousin Cocaine," "Brown Sugar" — referring to the mixture of heroin with strychnine and caffeine — and "Silver Lady," which means a hypodermic needle. The Stones produced their Black & Blue album in 1975. The jacket of the album featured pictures of a bruised and battered woman tied up in bondage style. The graphic was advertised on thousands of billboards in every major American city.

Then there's "acid rock," whose name speaks for itself. Thousands of adoring copy-cat fans, imitating their heroes, died of overdoses. Those that didn't die, the "punk rockers," dyed their hair green and disfigured themselves with vulgar tattoos or by putting rings or safety pins through their noses. Considered taboo in any previous male culture, bands such as KISS or the Sex Pistols convinced thousands of young males that this outright self-mutilation was "cool." KISS stands for "Knights in the Service of Satan," by the way.

Today's "heavy metal" rockers simply crawl with invitations to satanic cults, suicide, and murder. For those who still doubt the accuracy of these charges, check out the group Slayer, which provided background music for Tim Hunter's horror film River's Edge. The film is about the motiveless murder of a young girl, whose corpse is left lying naked beside a river.

The lyrics to one of Slayer's songs, "Hell Awaits," are set to a background of deafening loud drumbeats and howling guitars. Satan calls upon his legions to kill God and as many humans as possible. Another song, "Kill Again," is more explicit:

Lurking in the dismal fog/ hungry for your blood/ seeking harmless victims/ just kill and kill again.../ slice her flesh to shreds/ watch her blood flow free/ kill the preacher's only son/ watch the infant die/ bodily dismemberment/ drink the purest blood.

Then there's "Necrophilic":

Relentless lust of rotting flesh/ to trash the tomb she lies/ heathen whose of Satan's wrath/ I spit at your demise.../ I feel the urge the growing need/ to --- this sinful corpse/ my tasks complete the bitch's soul/ lies raped in demonic lust.

Young people are whipped into a frenzy at concerts conducted by groups such as the Slayers. They leap onto the stage. Attack the musicians. Hurl lengths of iron, coins, sharp-bladed knives at them. Some are stomped to death. Drugs such as the hallucinogenic LSD are passed around, are slipped into bottles of Coca-Cola, quickly turning unsuspecting victims into raving psychotics. Some even commit suicide.

A number of serial killers are zealous fans of heavy metal groups. The Mansons, for instance. Richard Ramirez, the Night Stalker, who murdered 10 people, swore by the AD-DC group. His role model was probably the "Night Prowler" in the album Highway to Hell. When arrested, and later on trial, Ramirez leaped to his feet, shouting: "Hail, Satan!"

Sad to say, but most — if not all — rock performers are very depraved individuals. But they are mere puppets, too, acting out a script. Modern electronic music, which came about in the early 1960s, is an element of cultural subversion.

Rock groups are heavily immersed in dangerous drugs, as are many of their compatriots in the film industry. Musicians and movie stars, and now many in the athletic field, are driven to popping uppers and downers.

John Lennon, the Beatles, the Rolling Stones, KISS, all were heroin addicts. Keith Richards had to have blood transfusions, replacing his entire heroin-laced blood supply, in order to appear drug free, so that he might get a visa to enter the United States.

These "rock stars" are nothing more than media creations. Behind-the-scene controllers fabricate their music. Remember when the Beatles arrived in the U.S. in 1964? The media announced that "Beatlemania" has invaded America, offering as evidence the screaming, writhing mass of young females swooning at their every utterance. But these frenzied girls had been recruited from a school in the Bronx and paid a handsome stipend to do their thing. And what a performance they put on.

Finally, these rock groups who made an untold fortune beyond estimating were completely under the thumbs of the mafia-connected promoters. The Rolling Stones, as a prime example, made over $200 million, yet they barely received enough money to survive on. They had no idea where their money had gone.

The Beatles

The Beatles got their start in the seedy dives of England and East Germany where prostitution and the circulation of drugs were rampant. They worked strip clubs for 10 shillings, strumming their guitars while an overaged woman bared all her assets for a bunch of drunk and rowdy sailors as well as guilt-ridden businessmen whose laps were covered by topcoats.

Finally, in 1960, the Lads from Liverpool got a booking at a jazz club in Hamburg's notorious Reeperbahn district. The clubs featured red lit windows occupied by whores decked out in all types of bizarre costumes, representing every age from nymphet to granny.

Far from the later image of innocence foisted on the gullible youth of the world, the Beatles stayed high on Preludin sometimes, even on stage, foaming at the mouth.

Lennon would often pop his cork, prancing, groveling, singing in unintelligible gibberish, except when he broke into cries of "Seig Heil" and streams of vulgarities and profanities.

On the street, Lennon and company were just as obnoxious, sometimes taunting churchgoers from the balcony of their hotel suite. Lennon attached a water-filled contraceptive to an effigy of Jesus and hung it out in full view of the people on their way to worship at St. Joseph's. Another time, he urinated down on the heads of three nuns.

The openly homosexual Brian Epstein signed the boys to a contract. He immediately set about creating a new image for them. The Beatles were scrubbed, washed, and their shoulder-length hair trimmed into the Beatles cut. EMI, one of Europe's largest recording producers, created the Beatles in their studio.

After changing their grooming habits, next came the monumental task of dealing with the Beatles' total lack of musical ability. The Lads could neither read music or play any instrument besides the guitar. One EMI producer called their musicianship "a bad joke." Someone had to sit in for Ringo on their first recording, cracking, "That guy (Ringo) couldn't do a drum roll to save his life."

EMI manufactured the whole myth of the Beatles' great European popularity, concocting wild stories of fans by the thousands rioting wherever the boys showed up. Front page stories told of police fighting to restrain a mob of over 1,000 squealing teenagers, even cropping photographs, showing only a handful of kids (all paid performers) who were supposedly the fringes of a huge throng of adoring fans. A photographer said later: "At most, there were six or seven girls."

More carefully staged demonstrations followed at Kennedy Airport when the Lads from Liverpool invaded the U.S. For an unprecedented two Sundays in a row, on the very popular Ed Sullivan Show, over 75 million Americans watched the very beginnings of a new phenomenon: the shaking of heads and swaying of bodies in a ritual that would soon be replicated by an untold number of rock groups.

The Brits, not to let a good thing go unnoticed, were upon their return home promptly inducted into the order of chivalry by the aristocracy. They were greeted, in fact, by no less than

Queen Elizabeth at Buckingham Palace.

Rolling Stones

Another rock group came into prominence about the same time as the Beatles: The Rolling Stones, featuring Mick Jagger and Keith Richards. They were the counterpart to the Lads from Liverpool. The Stones were "mean," "dirty," and "rebellious," whereas the Beatles were portrayed as the well-groomed "Fab Four." Kinda like pro "wrestling," where you have the "good guys" and the "bad guys," where, actually, they are merely two sides of the same coin. In fact, the Beatles composed the Stones' first hit record, and Beatle George Harrison made all the arrangements for their first recording contract. The Stones decided to emulate the path taken by the Beatles, but were disappointed when their first appearance on England TV met with negative reviews. Viewers called them "long-haired louts, absolutely disgusting."

But Stones' manager Andrew Oldham was in ecstasy at the ire displayed by TV viewers. "We're going to make you exactly opposite of those nice, clean, tidy Beatles. And the more parents hate you, the more kids will love you. Just you wait and see." The Stones, dutifully, followed the script, tearing apart the TV studio when they appeared on Ed Sullivan's Show. A grim-faced Sullivan told his audience, "I promise you, they will never be back on the show." But they had gotten just the results wanted. Their record sales immediately jumped into the millions.

The building blocks were firmly in place. Now they would be the means to transform an entire generation into heathen followers of the New Age, followers who could be molded into the future cadre of the satanic movement and then deployed into our schools, law enforcement agencies, churches, and political leadership.

Manson — Woodstock

1969 brought us Woodstock, the Manson murders, Altamont, and a nation recoiling from the assassinations of Martin Luther King, Jr. and Robert Kennedy, along with the stalemated war in Vietnam. Man would fly to the moon that year, but many of America's youths preferred to soar even higher on hallucinatory drugs to the sounds of acid rock.

The hippies proclaimed the dawning of a new age: "The Age of Aquarius," put to music by the Fifth Dimension. The age of Dionysus was upon us.

But Woodstock was more like the beginning of the end to youthful drug-induced optimism than the dawning of a new age. Jim Hendrix (1942-1970) himself was soon to become a symbol of the end. The talented black guitarist overdosed in September 1970, drowning in his own vomit, this shortly after making the claim that the culture he symbolized was "a new beginning."

Woodstock seems to be burned into the collective memory of the 1960s for Americans. But little is said of the disastrous concert at Altamont, California, which followed Woodstock. There, in full view of the rock stars and huge audience alike, members of the Hell's Angels murdered an 18-year-old black man who came to the concert with a white girl. Mick Jagger of the Stones, decked out as Lucifer in a red cape, had just sung his theme song: "Sympathy for the Devil."

Swaggering on stage, the gaunt, bleary-eyed Jagger sang:

Please allow me to introduce myself/ I'm a man of wealth and taste/ I've been around for a long long year/ Stole many a man's soul and faith/ I was around when Jesus Christ had his moment of doubt and pain/ made damn sure that Pilate washed his hands and sealed his fate.

**Pleased to meet you, hope you guess my
name/ But what's puzzling you is the nature of
my game. /Stuck around St. Petersburg when
I thought it was time for a change./ Killed the
Czar and his ministers, Anastasia screamed in
vain./ I rode a tank in the General's rank,/ When
the Blitzkrieg raged, and the fighting stank./**

**I watched with glee while all you kings and
queens/ authenticate for the gods they made./
I shouted out who killed the Kennedys,/ When
after all, it was you and me./**

**Just as every cop is a criminal and all sinners
saints/ As Hex is Tail Just Call me Lucifer/
Cause I'm in need of some restraint./**

**So if you meet me have some courtesy/ and
some sympathy and some taste./ Give all your
well-earned politics/ Or I'll lay your soul to
waste./**

Jagger sited Aleister Crowley, the Master Occult Magician of the 20th Century, as his mentor. The Beatles, the Rolling Stones, the Mamas and Papas, all of the rock performers of the 1960s and 1970s, sang the praises of Satan and were very close to the Mansons, as well as being members of the New Age Process Church. John Lennon even went so far in 1966 that he made the following statement to the international press: "Christianity will go. It will go. It will vanish and shrink. I needn't argue about that. I'm right and I will be proved right. We are more popular than Jesus now."

Mick Jagger and the Stones, not to be outdone, played a role in the making of the film Lucifer Rising. The film, made in England, also featured the Process Church and the Manson Family Cult. Marianne Faithful went all the way to Egypt to take part in the Black Mass scene, with the part of Lucifer depicted by Bobby Beausoleil, a member of the Mansons currently serving a life sentence for his part in the gruesome California ritualistic murders.

Anita Pallenberg, girlfriend of one of the Rolling Stones, became an ardent satanist. Some of her many male lovers called her a witch. "She was obsessed with Black Magic and began to carry a string of garlic with her everywhere — even to bed — to ward off vampires. She also had a strange mysterious old shaker for Holy Water which she used for some of her rituals. Her ceremonies became increasingly secret, and she warned me never to interrupt her when she was working on a spell. In her bedroom she kept a huge, ornately carved chest, which she guarded so jealously that I assumed it was her drug stash. The house was empty one day, and I decided to take a peep inside. The drawers were filled with scraps of bone, wrinkled skin and fur from some strange animals. She even stopped one day at the scene of an automobile accident in order to sop up the blood of the victim, which I suppose she believed to have occult powers."

In 1967, the Stones openly saluted Lucifer in an album titled Their Satanic Majesties Request, this following hard on the heels of the Beatles celebrating drugs: "Sargent Pepper's Lonely Heart Club Bank." In it, the Fab Four took a fantasized LSD trip, called "Lucy in the Sky with Diamonds," or LSD for short.

The album was a tribute to their late friend, Aleister Crowley on the 20th anniversary of his death. It began: "It was 20 years ago today." Crowley's picture was featured on the album's cover.

Shortly, thereafter, Lennon, on behalf of the Lads, boldly announced that the Beatles were regular takers of LSD. Paul McCartney said, "LSD opened my eyes. We use only one-tenth of our brain." They also began to plug for the legalization of marijuana. Some mild protest followed, including the banning of the album in Maryland by Gov. Spiro T. Agnew.

The war against American youth was escalated in 1967. Mass, open-air rock concerts were boisterously attended by over four million youngsters over the next two years, and the drugs began to flow like water through a busted damn. And not just pot or the lethal LSD, but new hallucinogenic drugs such as PCP, STP, and others. All of these were distributed free at these concerts, and millions of them returned home proclaiming the birth of a new culture and a "New Age."

Over 100,000 young people attended "The First Annual Monterey International Pop Festival," the real purpose of which was to introduce the kids to the mind-altering experience of LSD.

The hallucinogenic drug had first been used in the early 1960s in the Haight-Ashbury section of San Francisco. A CIA-British intelligence task force code-named MK-Ultra distributed 5,000 tablets of LSD through a commune known as Ken Kesey's Merry Pranksters. Kesey, a sometime poet and convicted felon, became famous for driving around California in a gaily painted bus with his commune, the Merry Pranksters, doling out LSD-laced Kool Aid wherever they stopped along the way.

The unsuspecting victims, after imbibing LSD, often became psychotic and unable to discern reality from their wild drug-induced hallucinations. Soon this psychosis became known simply as "a bad trip." Many young people committed suicide. Some suffered brain damage.

The popular group The Mamas and The Papas organized the festival at Monterey. Their lead, John Phillips, was a drug pusher and had close ties to Charles Manson and his satanists, as well as director Roman Polanski. Monterey's board of directors included Andrew Oldham (Rolling Stones manager), Mick Jagger, Beatle Paul McCartney, and Terry Melcher, the son of Doris Day.

Demonic groups such as The Who and drug-addict Jimi Hendrix made their American debut at Monterey. The Who ended their bizarre performance by destroying all their guitars, amplifiers, and drums. Hendrix simulated masturbation with his guitar on stage while performing at ear-shattering volume levels.

LSD was everywhere. "Monterey Purple" was passed out to everyone, yet the police, standing nearby, made no arrests, setting a precedent for future outdoor concerts.

This was the dawning of the "Age of Aquarius." And the end of the "Age of Pisces." History's largest happening. The age of Jesus Christ had come to an end. This multitude of brainwashed, drug-saturated youngsters at Monterey, Altemont, and Woodstock saw themselves as the vanguard of a new time, a Kairos time, a veritable paridigm - shift in the world. And while these isolated, filthy, drug-pumped youth wallowed in mud, copulating like bitch dogs in heat, the FBI and government officials did not try to stop them.

The origins of Woodstock are revealing. Artie Kornfield gave birth to the idea. He was the director of Capitol Records Contemporary Projects Division. The funding came from a large pharmaceutical company, while Sandoz Laboratories, the Swiss-based company that synthesized LSD, also provided funds.

The preparations for Woodstock were woefully inadequate; one might even say criminal. Half a million were expected, yet the food and water needed for such a throng were obviously in short supply. The sanitary facilities were a disgrace. Pumped up with drugs, the unruly mass of unkempt, unruly youth soon turned into a angry mob.

The Hog Farm, a hippie commune, provided security at Woodstock. Their leader, Wavy Gravy, a former member of Ken Kesey's MK-Ultra operation, the Merry Pranksters, was, along with his cohorts, a member of various Satanic cults, including the Process Church and Charley Manson's group. One groupie, Diane Lake, was a Manson member at the time of Sharon Tate's gory murder.

A 350-member security group, all off-duty New York City cops, bailed out on the festival 24 hours before it was set to begin. Woodstock was in big trouble as half a million kids swarmed into Woodstock protected only by the pitiful Hog Farm hippies.

Everyone knew the Hog Farm was a bunch of druggies, but Director John Roberts felt they were qualified to do the job of security. "After all," he reasoned, "they're wise in the way of drugs. They know good acid from bad, good trips from bummers, good medicine from poison."

The D.A. agreed. "There will be no arrests or prosecutions for violations of drug laws," he announced. And he kept his word!

50,000 kids flooded Woodstock a full two days prior to the festival. Drugs immediately surfaced. Some wag commented: "The tots swam naked, smoked grass, and got into the music." 99% of those attending smoked pot, according to a New York Times poll. But not a single arrest was made. One deputy quipped; "Where would we put all of them?"

Marijuana was bad enough, but a mere trifle compared to the Coca-Cola laced LSD being passed around. One cop drank some of this brew to relieve himself from the broiling heat, ignorant to the potent stuff spicing his soft drink. He was finally led away from his traffic directing post when his wild signals created a mega-logjam at the entrance to Woodstock.

Drugs and ear-shattering music wafted over the countryside for the next three days, as the high-as-a kite throng wallowed about in the knee-deep mud caused by torrential rains. There were no shelters. No way out. Autos and bikes had been parked eight miles away. But the music never stopped blaring and the bodies seldom ceased gyrating.

Many kids became violently ill, perhaps over 300 in the first 24 hours. They were on "bad" LSD trips. One festival announcer tried to issue a warning that badly manufactured acid (a term for LSD) was being circulated. "You aren't taking poison," he feebly warned. "It's just some bad stuff. You aren't going to die. . . . But if you're worried just take half a tablet." And who gave that lame duck advice? None other than Wavy Gravy, the MK-Ultra agent.

Things got worse. Kids were falling right and left. An emergency call to New York sent over 50 doctors rushing to the site. In all, they treated 5,000 violently sick kids.

The last major rock "festival" of the 1960s was held at Altemont racetrack outside San Francisco, featuring the Rolling Stones. It was Ken Kesey's idea.

And what an idea. It turned into a literal Satanic orgy, leaving four people dead and scores of others battered and bruised. Mick Jagger, lead singer of the Stones, played the role of Lucifer. The performance marked the beginning of the "heavy metal" concerts of today.

Over 400,000 attended Altemont, wallowing in drugs and sexual orgies, tripping out on acid, freaking out, sipping on cheap California wine, stoned out on Mexican grass and amphetamines. One guy was almost killed when he tried to fly from a speedway bridge. Another tumbled into a deep drainage ditch while his stoned-out friends reclined nearby with bemused smiles pasted on their chalky faces. No one seemed sure if it was real or a hallucination as the poor fellow sank beneath the surface. No matter, he was dead anyway. Meanwhile, doctors were kept busy delivering babies to girls having hysterical premature births. They were descending into a man-made Hell, and it continued for days on end. The Hell's Angels were supposed to be the security guards for the concert, ostensibly working for free beer, but getting their real payoff from the sale of drugs. The Angels were comprised of robbers, rapists, murderers, and drug-addicts.

Mick Jagger, almost two hours tardy, put on quite a show. He came on stage dressed in a satin cape, which glowed red under the lights. He was Lucifer.

Now followed a bizarre spectacle. With Jagger prancing about, several kids rose up in the audience, stripped off their clothes and crawled on stage as though it were a high altar, there to offer themselves as victims for the boots and cues of the Angels. The more they were beaten and bloodied, the more they were impelled, as if by some supernatural force to offer themselves as human sacrifices to these agents of

Satan. Now they needed a real human sacrifice. And they had one: a black man named Meredith Hunter, who stood in front of the stage with his girlfriend.

Mick Jagger, introducing himself as Lucifer, began singing "Sympathy for the Devil," which was to become the number one hit record in America. The entire audience arose as one, breaking into a frenzied dance. Suddenly, one of the Angels, a hairy, six-foot-four behemoth, tried to provoke a fight with the black man, yanking his hair violently. Some jostling ensued. Five more Angels rushed to the aid of their cohort while Meredith tried vainly to run away. An Angel plunged a knife into the black man's head, but the blade didn't penetrate deeply. Meredith panicked. He whipped a pistol out and fired it point-blank at one of the Angels. Now the Angels attacked all out, tearing the pistol form his hand, stabbing him in the face, chest, and all over his body. Meredith crumpled to the ground a bloody mess. Several people rushed forward to render aid, but the Angels locked arms and stood guard over the motionless body of the black man. One of the goons shouted, "He's going to die anyway, so just let him die."

No gun was ever found on Meredith. No one was ever indicted. No one stepped forward as a witness, probably because they feared retaliation from the Angels.

Even while the terrible fight went on, the Stones continued paying homage to the devil. Finally, Jagger did try to restore order, "Cool out. Just cool out, and take it easy," an obviously terrified Jagger pleaded over the mike. But they just ignored him. The black man was dead, and incredibly the entire tragic incident had been caught on film, which was released throughout the country as Gimme Shelter. Was it all preplanned? Or just a terrible accident? Jagger later compared the staging and effects of the Stones' concerts to huge Nazi rallies of the late 1930 captured on film by Lennie Reichenstahl, entitled Triumph of the Will. Gimme Shelter, a box office hit, can still be purchased or rented today at many video stores.

1969 also saw the debut of Ozzy Osbourne, a member of the Black Sabbath group, which modeled itself on their idols, the Rolling Stones. For the next 15 years, way into the 1980s, a succession of young drugged-out performers like Osbourne competed for the "big money" and lucrative recording contracts. The keys to their ultimate success: the ability to portray decadence and evil. These were the "heavy metal" bands.

Hazekiah Ben Aaron, now a devout Christian was once a member of the Church of Satan. He gave an interview to New Solidarity in 1985, in which he revealed that such "heavy metal" groups such as Black Sabbath, The Blue Oyster Cult, The Who, Ozzy Osbourne, and many others were all spawned by the Church of Satan under the direction of Anton LaVey. Others claim that LaVey was just a front man for Kenneth Anger, the man who recruited the Rolling Stones to the occult.

In 1985, Ben Aaron said in an interview: "I was working for the Church (of Satan) . . . they also had people who were middlemen for other companies. They were middlemen for Apple (set up by the Beatles), Warner Brothers, and other record companies . . . "

Michael Aquino and Anton LaVey both expressed a thorough dislike for rock music, but they operated at a higher level as Satanic controllers than the mind-corrupting rock performers that they deployed. Aquino was also adept at acoustical brainwashing methods. In January 1989, the Satanic network, Thelma Net, made available an article Aquino had written several years earlier, entitled "Magic and Machines." Here are some excerpts:

If we begin to study the complex ideas and concepts that are inherent in legitimate Satanism, we are always surprised and interested to hear of the use of electro-mechanical methods for influencing the atmosphere in the immediate interior of ritual space. Ionization, ozonization, high-frequency

resonance, and electromagnetic fields are all employed in the rooms of magicians. . . . The introduction of these energies . . . serves a double purpose. The first is to increase the physical cleansing of the ritual room from the exterior world. The second is the cerebral cleansing of the participants who are in the immediate zone of influence in the ritual room. The most well-known source of information on this special form of black magic is Dr. Anton Szandor LaVey's book Satanic Rituals. . . .

In addition to the energies that appear in a electrical high voltage field, sound waves of high frequency and especially lighting effects and the configuration of the room contribute to desired alienation. The Temple of Set has for years researched these little-known areas of black magic. Our work has been in general successful. A Southern California firm has recently brought onto the market equipment that, with the help of light flashes and definite sound frequencies, produces the desired waves in the human brain for purposes of relaxation. It is rather interesting to note that German magicians employed the same techniques over 80 years ago. . . .

Binaural heat is produced by tuning so that each ear will hear a slightly different frequency; for example, one ear might hear a signal at 440 Herz and the other at 434. A 6-Hz beat would be produced which would be heard as if in one's own head. These beats are perceived even at extraordinary low amplitudes—perhaps as low as a hundred times below the auditory threshold. Certainly, the perception of such a beat can disorient the hearers and render them highly suggestible.

Colonel Aquino's professional career, remember, was military intelligence. Some of the same acoustical warfare was probably used against David Kourish, Manuel Noriega in Panama, and the papal nuncio.

He wrote an article in 1988 titled "Music That Kills," which was a report on a multi-wave oscillator (MWO). The unit was sold for $700 by the New Age electronics firm Klark Kent Science of Dayton, Ohio.

The MWO emitted a band of radio frequencies that reached from the audible spectrum up to microwaves and beyond. Aquino theorizes that with this multiplicity of frequencies, all the living cells in an 'irradiated' individual can be excited in their special cell resonances to a higher biological activity. An independent researcher, who remained with the field for more than one hour, reports that everything went black and he had to "break off the experiment so as to not lose consciousness."

Today's Popular Music

The top selling 20 albums in America as the century turned were rap, all of which had parental-advisory stickers. Most of this rap "music" (which is really pure rhythm, spoken rather than sung) are outrageous and violent. Example: Ice Cube's "The Nigga You Love to Hate," rappin' about terminating an unwanted pregnancy by beating his woman in the belly. Or, for another example, "The Mind of a Lunatic" by Geto Boys:

> **Her body's beautiful, so I'm thinkin' rape./**
> **Shouldn't have had her curtains open so that's**
> **her fate./**
> **She begged me not to kill her, I gave her a rose,/**
> **Then slit her throat and watched her shake till**
> **her eyes closed./**
> **Had sex with her corpse before I left her . . . /**

We would not dare to print the vile filth spewing from such moronic groups as Live Crew (As Nasty as They Wanna Be).

Tupac Shakur ("Strictly 4 My N.I.G.G.A.Z") boasted, "I'd rather use my gun 'cause I get the money quicker -- got 'em in the frame - Bang! Bang! -- blowing mutha _ _ _ to the moon."

Even worse (can that possibly be?) is Eminem who boasts about slitting his mother's throat and deflowering his sister on her birthday, and other sexual atrocities too hideous to repeat.

The lyrics from such groups as Live Crew have been described as "sado-sud," where the word bitch has become a mantra. Ice Cube used it fifty-seven times in one album.

Taking cues from these vile excretions has been the movies, particularly those of Quentan Tarantino, but also in films such as GoodFellas Cook/Thief, Henry-Serial Killer, Pulp Fiction, etc., all of which are saturated with vulgarity, violence, and hatred of women.

A courageous black woman, Delores Tucker, has spoken out against what she calls "pornographic smut, which black children embrace as role models — Children want to dress like them, walk like them, talk like them, and use language that you wouldn't believe. This is the filth that our children are buying — this is pornography, and every kid is saying these words now."

Blacks and whites in ever increasing numbers are speaking out against this insidious brainwashing of American youth, especially teens of African-American background.

Another example: The music soundtrack from Blue Streak is nothing more than a celebration of criminality.

Without question (despite those who adamantly remain Doubting Thomases), there is a direct relationship between a) violent attacks on women and b) much of so-called popular music, especially gangsta-rap.

The abuse and exploitation of women has been going on throughout recorded history, so we are not suggesting that this is an unprecedented social phenomenon. We are saying that the hatred of women in music is a new thing, unheard of during the Golden Age of popular music, when timeless standards were being crooned by the likes of Perry Como, Bing Crosby, Doris Day, Rosemary Clooney, and Jo Stafford.

Most adults simply haven't a clue as to what our youth (and some adults, for that matter) are listening to. I give you this advice: LISTEN TO IT. Force yourself, if you must, but DO IT.

Also, let's not delude ourselves that all this is peculiar to America. It is still a practice in Asia for parents to kill their newborn babies if they are female. The notion that women might be granted equal rights in Muslim cultures is considered a satanic plot. In other parts of the world, males often kill a relative if she has been raped.

All these are cruel and savage acts which we here in American rightly condemn. Yet, here in the United States, we have a popular music industry that vigorously supports, encourages, and profits by such atrocities. Nowhere else in the world is this allowed! Said one observer: "The idiots who ripped the clothes off women in Central Park were raised on gangsta-rap and aggro-rock. It did not reflect their world view, it formed it."

Unfortunately, many black entertainers and social critics at first defended rap stars and their musical excrement. But some members of the Africo-American community are finally (if belatedly) beginning to see the light, calling the music sheer barbarism.

Whites, too, have fallen right into the trap, purchasing just as many (if not more) rap albums than their black counterparts.

MTV helped guide the popular music industry into the sewer, providing a platform for the sexually-deviant performances of Madonna (and all of her actions are an insult to that lofty name). Now we have the likes of Britney Spears, shamelessly exposing herself, acting more like an exotic dancer at some Bourbon Street strip joint than a popular entertainer.

Popular music of my day (WWII Era) gave us the big bands of Glenn Miller, Artie Shaw, Tommy Dorsey, Duke Ellington, Count Basie, and Guy Lombardo — music that will live forever. The immortal lyrics of Sammy Kahn, Irving Berlin, Cole Porter, and so many others. The singers we mentioned before, along with Ella Fitzgerald, Nat "King" Cole, Sarah Vaughn, and the unforgettable music of B.B. King, "Satchmo" Louis Armstrong, and the incomparable Sammy Davis, Jr., not to mention Harry Bellafonte.

Square? Corny? Maybe. But all of them played danceable music, and the lyrics exalted women. Hey, I fell in love with my wife to the playing of Hogey Carmichael's "Stardust." Pray they never stop writing songs about lonely GI's missing their girlfriends, guys falling in love, and fellas lamenting "The One That Got Away."

Video Games

Long before Columbine, there were dozens and dozens of violent incidents and killings in high schools and neighbor-hoods. On December 1, 1977, in Paducah, Kentucky, the 14-year-old Michael Corneal took six guns to school and shot and killed three girls: Jessica James, Kayce Stegner, and Nicole Marie Hadley. He wounded five others. Corneal was an avid computer user who was constantly in search of violent and obscene movies on the Internet. His favorite movies? Basketball Diaries and Natural Born Killers.

Corneal's favorite computer game was "Doom," which is based on a pattern of moving quickly from one target to another with an emphasis on head shots. This 14-year-old boy, who had never before used a firearm, hit eight people with eight bullets on that fateful day in Paducah. Five were struck in the head, three in the torso. The parents of the three murdered girls are engaged in a lawsuit with the producers of these satanic video games and movies. Their suit claims that Basketball Diaries represents a nihilistic glamorization of irresponsible sex, senseless and gratuitous violence, hatred of religion, disregard of authority, castigation of family, drug use, and other self-destructive behavior, and that, therefor, it is a harmful influence on impressionable minors.

Colonel David Grossman, who teaches courses on the psychology of killing to the Green Berets and Federal agents, point out that point-and-shoot video games have the same effect as military training techniques used to break down a soldier's aversion to killing. These video games, says Grossman, "are even more powerful than military training games." So the United States has now purchased a version of "Doom" to train their soldiers.

Role playing and the creation of a plot with characters is often incorporated into some games. What makes these games unlike any other form of media violence is that the viewer is not passive but is IN the movie. You do not just watch John Claude Van Damme blow someone away. YOU pull the trigger. If you get killed yourself, the game is over, and the only way to remain master of this intoxicating new universe IS TO KILL!

Daikatana adds a new dimension, taking advantage of the roaring processing speed of computers and powerful three-dimensional graphics acceleration cards. You, the viewer — the participant — are sitting in a chair, operating a mouse and a keyboard. The computer field replaces your field of vision and you believe you are actually creeping around a corner, afraid the enemy is lying in wait. Your pulse goes into overdrive. The monster leaps out at you, causing a great rush of adrenaline through your body. You can almost feel the wet blood.

What are the makers of this game up to? Harmless fun? I'm afraid not. Instead, this is a very conscious policy. The media — Hollywood — is out to dehumanize the population, to desensitize human beings, and to develop the idea that when you shoot, an automatic reaction sets in before you even have time to make a moral choice about what you do. The automatic reaction of the four policemen who pumped 41 shots into Diallo (in New York), an unarmed man, was a result of the same kind of police training that kids are being fed hour after hour in these video games. It is inevitable that killing an object, over and over, time after time, will eventually become your second nature.

Eric Harris had worked up to 100 hours programming the "Doom" video game to make it more or less explicitly the plan for his attack at Columbine High School. Investigators of the

Simon Wiesenthal Center in Los Angeles concluded that he had incorporated the Columbine school floor plan into the game. So Harris had also to be in a "God" mode, in which the player is invincible.

Pokemon — The Cult

There is a bug which is infesting the minds of millions of children in American. Yet 99% of the parents are clueless. The bug's name is Pokemon.

What values does Pokemon teach? For openers, that fighting is good because you have more power to smash your enemy.

One Pokemon would be enough to frighten anyone, but there are actually 150 Pokemons. Pokemon is the short form of "pocket monster." These different monsters have different powers, so you can play a game, a newer game, called a stadium game, where they have a big screen and 20 smaller screens, and mesmerized little tykes and their parents are enthusiastically playing the game. The central idea is you select six Pokemons and you have your fighting techniques.

Pick six or so of the 150 Pokemons, and you have four types of weapons in this particular game (there are other games, of course), and then you can attack your opponent either through fire (you throw fire at them), or electricity, lightning, or you destroy them through seismic shock, and eventually you subdue your opponent.

All of it is quite mechanistic; there is no way to influence the game, other than this mechanistic button-pushing. No cognition is involved as everyone is reduced to the level of a Pavlovian dog. Maybe less. A Pavlovian dog at least is fed something to eat in the beginning.

Here are some of the things you see on Fox TV every afternoon:

Sounds of crashing, smashing, screaming:

"Mommy, mommy."

47

Electronically amplified voice over loudspeakers:

"Out next match is between Hit and Steel Dude, and Steel Dude is hard as a rock. Yo, Dude, this time Hit???"

Sounds of crashing and thudding.

Female voice: "Don't show any mercy! Kick, Kick, Kick, Kick."

More sounds of electronic music thumping and pounding. Unintelligible yelling. Screaming, sounds of engines vrroomming.

Adult voice: "You did it"

Kid's voice: "All right!"

More horrible sounds of voices; one voice cuts in:

"What are you doing? Kick, kick."

Voice resembling that of Donald Duck: "Your secret weapon is ready!"

"All you gotta do now is use this remote control."

"Have Hit jump up and then flip the switch. One hundred thousand volts will run through the ring followed by an explosion."

Maniacal laughter.

"One thing's wrong."

Unintelligible screaming.

Kid's voice: "All right! Use the seismic guns now."

Crashing, screaming.

Kid's voice: "We did it!"

Horrible noises.

"We did it!"

Sounds of audience cheering.

"It's been quite a while since he sent me a new Pokemon. I wonder what he's captured this time?"

"What is that smell?"

Horrible noises, running water, panting and gasping.

"We could have suffocated."

Donald Duck voice: "The city has been plunged into darkness by a power failure."

"A power failure is it? I can identify with failure."

This is the type of trash shown daily on Fox TV during the children's programming, and latchkey children and thousands of others are tuned in. And the Pokemon industry is all around us, from tee-shirts to bed sheets, watches, and all types of clothing and ornamentation.

The minds of 3-year-old children are being poisoned by this stuff. Check this out. In one Pokemon cartoon we find a young girl, Sabrina, who is violently attacked by the Dream-Eater. This is a gas Pokemon which sucks out the opponent's soul. In another, a high-level haunter appears suddenly, steals people's souls, and vanishes. The kids in the show immediately plan an all-out counterattack, vowing revenge.

And what about poor Sabrina? Well, they say, "Who would have thought that such a sweet girl like her would become so consumed with the desire for revenge? The haunter may have eaten her soul, but she's still able to tell us where she is through telepathy."

The minds of young children are immensely impression-able. They learn primarily through imitation and through play. And what do they learn to imitate from Pokemon? Aggression. Violence. Revenge. What they do not learn is love, compassion, joy, forgiveness, respect for self and others, truth, and tenderness.

Norbert Weiner poses a task in his book Cybernetics that one has to find a neurological mechanism, matching the theory of John Locke about the association of thought based on sensuous experience. Pokemon offers no hypothesis, no creativity, no soul, no cognition. The only soul-sucking monster around is the Dream-Eater Pokemon. It sucks the soul of an impressionable young child and turns that child into a potential killer — another Eric Harris.

The lawyer representing the three dead girls from Paducah, who is suing multiple video game and movie companies, has said, "We need a nuclear war against these people."

I don't agree with the violent terminology, but we definitely need to recognize the makers and peddlers of these violent games and movies as the backbone of the Culture of Death to which Pope John Paul II and others have been alluding.

The large issues we must deal with — the war games and these computer games — are based on the same method. We must oppose them with our prayers and our protests.

And beware of the Internet connections to our schools, for unless we have fundamental changes in the education system, the more little monsters we will create — and they are not going to be Pokemon monsters.

Says Colonel David Grossman of the world of video games, "They're using intense manipulation of screen imagery, colors, and rapid-fire imagery changes in order to make this a powerfully addictive substance for children. At the heart of the addictive substances is the violence."

There is no single factor, no magic bullet, if you will, in determining the ultimate cause of violence. Do poverty, gangs, drugs, rock music, easy access to firearms, child abuse, and family disintegration cause people to solve their problems with extreme acts of anti-social behavior? Of course, these are ALL important existing factors. If you take all of these factors, adding on the media violence — television, movies, pornography, and the violent video games — the result is a veritable explosion of violent crime, as evidenced in any nation where all of these factors are in place.

In our own beloved United Sates since 1967, for instance, per capita violent crime has risen six- to sevenfold. The murder rate would be astronomical but for the fact that medicine is able to save countless wounded victims who would have not so long ago died of their wounds. The assault rate, however, is horrendous, as more and more people every year are being shot, stabbed, and physically assaulted.

We all tend to look for simplistic answers to complex problems, so we blame it on the proliferation of guns. Certainly, it is extremely vital that we keep guns out of the hands of children. Even the ACLU and the NRA agree on this point, if nothing else. But even here, we walk on thin ice because kids will commit felonies to get guns. The Paducah, Kentucky, killer broke into a locked cabinet in a locked garage in a neighbor's house to acquire a firearm. The Littleton killers had pseudo-adults steal for them to get the guns they wanted. And the kids in Jonesboro, Arkansas, aged 11 and 13, used an acetylene torch in a failed gun theft attempt, then stole a car, finally using a crowbar to smash into a gun safe.

What about our neighbor to the north? Surely things are safer in Canada where strict gun laws have been in place for quite a while? In Canada's semi-socialistic arrangement, under the watchful eye of a paternalistic state, there is almost zero racial problems, yet since 1964, per capita violent crime has gone up fivefold, and attempted murders are up sevenfold.

So maybe in Europe? Afraid not. Violent crime in Norway has skyrocketed over the past 15 years. Same story in Greece, Australia, and New Zealand. Per capita crime has tripled during the same period in Sweden and has doubled in seven other European nations. Meanwhile in India, murders have doubled.

Now we come across an interesting — and revealing — set of facts. Television came to India in the early 1970s, closely followed by a significant rise in the murder rate. And there is this: Wherever American violent media has made inroads, the murder rate in those nations has practically doubled.

In Brazil and Mexico, violent crime has never been higher. Finally, there is Japan. Here is a nation with a homogeneous society, an intact family structure, universal employment, and draconian gun laws, yet, in 1977 alone, there was a 30% increase in juvenile violence. What we have here is a worldwide phenomenon.

So what should we do? Outlaw guns? That would be a start, but only a start. And that alone would not solve the deep underlying problem. Same thing with drugs. Banning drugs will not alleviate the problem anymore than treating a deep wound with peroxide and a bandaid, especially if we continue to glamorize drugs with nightly TV doses of action heroes shooting up drugs and smoking pot. The demand for drugs will, if this continues, far excel our ability to keep the poison off the streets.

No, passing more laws will not bring about the end of violence as long as we continue to glamorize violence and death and horror. And don't count on the media to give any straightforward, uncompromising information. What you'll get instead is misinformation, if not downright lies. Go instead to the major medical associations in the world, including our own Surgeon General. All of these prestigious medical groups have agreed on one salient point: **There is a direct link between media violence and violence in our society.**

Violence in movies leads to violence in our society. Television the same. And then there are the video games . .

Video games present a special problem. What we have here is a new product, and the makers of these games are claiming that the data on a direct link between media and societal violence does not apply to them — sorta like asserting that what applies to cigarettes does not hold true for cigars. Deny though they may, the facts indicate a strong link between the violent visual imagery these games portray and the violence flourishing all around us. Violence is a learned skill. It is learned through visual observation, and using a simulator is even more powerful than watching a training film.

Video games ARE simulators. Just as surely as a flight simulator can teach a person to fly, what we have in these violent video games are murder simulators. They have no redeeming social value whatsoever. They simply teach you how to kill. What if these were rape simulators? Do you suppose we would blithely allow our children to play them, much less sit in front of them for hours and hours? I think not. Yet, we let our kids play these violent video games for endless hours as they practice how to blow people's heads off — and parents are paying untold dollars for the "privilege" of having their children brainwashed and desensitized to their own humanity.

Some will obviously object by saying, "Hey, they're just kids playing games." Like when you were a kid, playing cops 'n robbers, firing away with your trusty cap gun or water pistol — "Bang, bang, Tommy, I got you. You're dead." And Tommy would jump up, guns blazing. "You missed me," he would yell. That would get your anger up 'cause Tommy was cheating. So just for good measure, you would belt him in the chops or kick him in the shins, sending him off bawling to mama. Then there would be hell to pay 'cause Tommy was real, and you hurt him, and mama just might retaliate with a hickory stick to your bottom.

We are no longer playing with wooden guns, however. In video game action, you can blow Tommy to smithereens. You can blow him away umpteen times, and you won't have to answer to an irate mother — or anyone else.

Maybe it's just that we don't understand the true purpose of play. Even in violent games of collision, such as rugby or football, when someone is injured, play stops. There are rules to follow, and a player is not allowed to go outside the rules, such as an elbow to the head or jumping on a player after the whistle has blown or when he is clearly out of bounds. No hitting below the belt or on the break. No intentionally head hunting by deliberately throwing at a batter. The purpose of the games is to play rough but within clearly proscribed rules of safety and sportsmanship. Players who go out of their way to injure others are considered renegades — criminals, really. And many ice hockey players and brawling baseball players have learned this lesson the hard way and had to pay the consequences for their errant behavior on the playing field. Video games offer no consequences for any errant behavior. The most beloved athletes in history were guys like Stan Musial, Lou Gehrig, Al Kaline, and Joe Montano, who always played with pride, dignity, self-restraint, self-effacing always, and always showing respect for their competitors. None of these character traits can be instilled or developed in our youth by use of today's video games.

These violent video games are identical to military-quality training devices. Killing for our soldiers becomes a conditioned response, turning off the safety catch. What do I mean by "safety catch"? It all goes back to World War II. At that time the military discovered the alarming fact that the vast majority of the U.S. soldiers did not want to fire in anger at the so-called enemy. This, they quickly deduced, could be traced back to the training given GIs in which they were taught to fire at bull's-eye targets. The superior weaponry given to soldiers proved quite accurate, but no bull's eye ever returned the fire. What was lacking was a real live target — a human being! Members of law enforcement and FBI trainees showed the U.S. military the way to solve the problem of soldiers not wanting to shoot other human beings. What they needed was a man-shaped silhouette for the trainees to shoot at that would, with practice and repetition, desensitize them to shooting at a human being, shooting to kill.

The same holds true for training a prospective pilot or a rig operator. If I want to teach you to fly, then we'd need a flight simulator. In this "machine," we can deal with stress and crisis as you man a most realistic flight simulator, and when you finally step into a real airplane, nothing is unfamiliar. So to teach you to kill, we need a killing simulator. In the military and in the law enforcement communities, the conditioned stimulus is a man-shaped silhouette that pops up in your field of view. You have but a split second to engage the target. If your aim is true, the target instantly drops. Stimulus-response. Stimulus-response. Repeat this same scenario over and over, hundreds of times, and when an enemy soldier pops up in front of you — boom! You shoot. You shoot to kill. No compunction. No hesitation. Just shoot. And in Vietnam, left to their own devices, GIs were much more willing to shoot than the soldiers in World War II.

According to David Grossman, something disturbingly similar happens to kids with violent video games. The kid pulls the trigger. He feels the recoil. He hits the target. The target drops. Not only does the youngster develop the mental skill to kill, but he also develops the physical ability to kill — the pointing skills and the trigger control that allowed the young boy in Paducah, Kentucky, to fire eight shots and score eight hits on eight different kids. Certainly, anyone who has ever fired a handgun or assault rifle will agree that this was something akin to supernatural accuracy.

Can we as a society not see that these violent video games are nothing more than murder simulators? And even worse than that, they are mass-murder simulators. In these games, the child drills and drills and drills some more. The drills are all designed to teach him to kill every living creature in front of him until he runs out of either bullets or targets.

In some many recent shooting involving young kids, the shooter initially set out to kill just one person — say a girlfriend — but kept on shooting every living creature that got in the way until they simply ran out of targets or were physically

55

stopped. Upon being questioned after the shootings, the kids said they just didn't know why they went on a shooting spree. The police were baffled. But the answer was right in front of them. These shooters had been drilled to kill every living creature who loomed in their path, and when the shooting began, the stimulus-response kicked in, and these kids literally went on "automatic pilot," doing the very thing they had been conditioned to do.

Make no mistake about it: The manufacturers of video games and producers of pornographically vicious movies are operating at the lowest possible moral level. They know these products are harmful to children, that children will gravitate to behavior that makes them feel powerful, but they will not accept any form of regulation because to do so would mean a smaller bottom line for them and their backers.

Colonel Grossman points out a salient fact: Violent visual images can be processed by a child by the tender age of 18 MONTHS! Imagine, a mere baby can know what's happening on the TV screen. They will not understand that it's not real until they're six, seven, or eight.

18 MONTHS! Straight into the eye and straight into the emotional center with great and powerful impact.

We'll close this section with the eloquent plea of Colonel Grossman, who witnessed the mass shootings at Jonesboro. "What we have here in front of us is a joint corporate moral responsibility, to reel in an industry that is systematically selling death and horror and destruction to our children. And around the world as each new level of violence is sold to the kids (and at young ages they suck this stuff up), 15 years later we see the impact. God only knows what the impact is going to be of what's being given to our kids now, but Paducah and Pearl and Littleton and Springfield are all an indication of what's in front of us. . . . And it's not going to stop until we stop teaching our kids to kill."

PART THREE

—

WHERE ARE OUR CHILDREN —
AND WHAT ARE THEY UP TO?

There are at this moment, in the year 2005, well over 2,000,000,000 children in the world. Their first task is quite formidable, namely being born at all. The total population of children under age 18 is shrinking, especially in Europe, by almost fifty percent. Birthrates have fallen somewhat in Africa, by nearly a third in Asia, and by almost half in North America. People, it seems, are becoming very reluctant to bring new life into the world.

Besides the difficulties of just being born, children are also dying at an alarming rate. Over 11,000,000 under age five died in 2000. A great portion of these youngsters come from underdeveloped countries, with only just over 60,000 coming from industrialized nations. That should be the norm for all countries, but most of the deaths will occur in the former Soviet Union, Ibero, the Mideast, and especially Africa.

What kills children? One of the major killers is war! Nearly 20% will die of diarrhea, which is caused directly from bad drinking water. Over 2,000,000 die in a single year because of the simple lack of infrastructure to deliver clean water and sanitation.

Most of the rest die from diseases that have been eradicated elsewhere, such as acute respiratory infections, perinatal disorders, noncommunicable diseases, measles, malaria. War takes 16%.

Basically we're dealing with two problems:

(1) There is a lack of good and sufficient medical attention in underdeveloped countries; medical services and medicine are desperately needed.

(2) Hunger. Children are dying of hunger and malnutrition in the underdeveloped countries. Malnutrition weakens them to the point that they cannot fight off disease.

WHAT ARE THEY UP TO? There are 1,600,000,000 school-aged children. Learning to simply read would be greatly beneficial to these kids because anyone not having basic reading skills is often left by the wayside. Besides, his potential as a human being is trampled when he is not educated. He is being robbed of his God-given right to develop his potentials to the max. Yet, woefully, over 400,000,000 children, a full 24%, are not in school.

More than 250,000,000 of the world's children are employed and expected to be the sole financial providers for their families. Hundreds of thousands toil as bonded laborers making carpets, hands chafed, sore, and often deformed. Bonded laborers put into servitude to pay a debt incurred by their parents. Children sold into debt bondage who work very long hours for many years to pay off debts. Children doing hazardous work deep beneath the surface of the earth in mining and construction. Many are severely injured or killed every year.

Work. Gruelling work. Work with scant pay, no benefits, and no free time. Work with no days off and no vacation. Girls working as domestic servants, often in bonded-labor situations. Working, quite often, just for their room and board. Girls suffering from sexual abuse.

Children working as vendors. Children begging for food and handouts. Children selling their bodies as sexual slaves.

"Ah," you'll say, "but we don't have anything comparable to that anymore in America. We did away with the sweat jobs and most of the abuses of the textile mills." Most, perhaps, but not all. But even if we had cleaned it all up, the question still arises: Are we in America living off the backs of child labor all over the world — which is represented by the United States' huge trade deficit?

Let's say you go to Wal-Mart and purchase a child's tee-shirt for $3. Check out the label. It might read something like the following: "Made in the Dominican Republic." That tee-shirt began its long journey to the U.S. in a hot cotton field. Then came the production of the cotton fabric, followed by the piecework to make the tee-shirt, and then the shipping. Each step of the journey brought with it yet another mark up in the ultimate retail price of the shirt — mark ups all the way to the Wal-Mart or K-Mart, yet it can be sold to you at the really economical price of $3. Doesn't seem possible, does it?

Look even closer and you'll discover that most of the clothes come from Bangladesh, which has the cheapest outsourcing for the garment industry in the world. Even Haiti, the Dominican Republic, et al, outsource to Bangladesh and have the clothes for their quota to export to America made there. They simply apply the label from their own country when they are ready to export them, but the $3 tee-shirts actually come from Bangladesh.

The average hourly wage of a unionized U.S. garment worker in 1970 was $8.71. In the year 2000, the same garment worker brings home (in constant dollar figures) somewhat less — $8.07. Sounds more like the turn of the 20th Century than the 21st, but the facts indicate that New York City is filled with illegal sweatshops where illegal immigrant workers are toiling for way below minimum wage — some as low as $.75 to $2.00 an hour — an average of $1.37. Terrible, indeed, and even worse in Bangladesh where children work for only $.03 an hour. There they work simply for enough wages to put a little food on the table at day's end. What can we call this form of work other than what it is: SLAVERY!

Many have argued against globalization on this very ground, arguing — rather persuasively — that free trade lowers the world's wages, destroying American jobs at the same time. Globalization must be replaced with a new monetary system and a new mission for development of the underdeveloped countries. This boils down to nothing short of a moral question, not one of economics per se, nor an objective problem of resources in the world. These are not purely objective problems but subjective political questions. Moral questions, no less. We must become responsible moral agents whose mission it is to help move humanity forward, or else bury our heads in the sands, pretending not to see more millions of children become slaves.

By the year 2010, there will be an estimated 10,000,000 AIDs orphans in Africa alone. There will be no schools for them to attend. The HIV virus is sweeping across Africa with all the devastation of the bubonic plague of the Middle Ages. The same is not true of America. Why? Is it because we have better sexual practices? Hardly! Africa is suffering with the AIDs epidemic because the population is physically depleted with immune systems that are running way overtime. A child is more likely to die of measles in Africa than a child in white suburban America. So will the AIDs orphan die quicker in Africa.

Then there are the 14,000,000 children around the world who live in camps for refugees or the internally displaced. Millions languish within miserable compounds without medical services, adequate food, sanitary conditions, or any educational programs.

War brings special problems and hell on earth for millions of children, such as the Rwandan Hutu refugees in Eastern Congo, slowly wasting away from starvation. They are homeless, their families systematically slaughtered in the Congo War of 1997.

One-third of the casualties of modern high-tech war are children. Ten million were killed in the 1990s alone. In Sudan, 12,000 children trekked through the southern part of that gutted land **FOR FOUR YEARS**. Four years without adult company. Four years until they finally arrived in Kenya, many being quickly recruited as fighters in Southern Sudan for John Garang's SPLA.

Street children — millions fending for themselves without families, without shelter. Every day these poor wretches face hunger, disease, poverty, violence, terror, and sexual abuse.

Forced to the streets by poverty-stricken families who cannot feed, clothe, or care for them, these kids present some of the saddest sights on earth. The powerful movie Saloom Bombay accurately depicted the terrible plight of the street kids of Bombay, India. These are the cast-off children of globalization. AIDs orphans by the hundred of thousands, 2% of Bombay's 9,000,000 population. They are vulnerable because of lack of security, thus creating physical, psychological, and social problems for the children. They truly lack a basis for survival. Food, money, shelter, clothes, and health care are all something they must often do without. Add to this the natural elements of cold, rain, floods, and the constant threat of wild beasts, in addition to insect and mosquito bites. On a smaller scale, thousands of children in the inner cities of America daily face similar problems. These are the people we often have turned our backs on in America.

Many kids not going to school are child prostitutes — over 1,000,000 of them alone in Asia. In Thailand, in the decimated rural sections of the country, it is an accepted practice for the daughter to go to the city and spend a period of time before she takes on a husband. And there is an ever-growing market, including in America, for child prostitution accounting for the rise in "missing children" and the European sex tours for child prostitution. (Christian Science Monitor)

The most criminal aspect of all these horror stories concerning children has to be the rise of the phenomenon of the child soldier. Here, by the hundreds of thousands, we see children being killed and their souls destroyed. At this moment, there are over 300,000 child soldiers on active duty from Sudan to Liberia to Columbia. Child soldiers are particularly ferocious fighters who take orders easily since they are malleable and quite psychologically vulnerable. Most are orphans who join the ranks of the Army seeking protection and food. Many, however, are forcibly recruited, taken away after their parents are killed. Thus the child who enters the ranks of insurgents is probably already traumatized and desperate. Though only a child, he quickly becomes a vicious killer, getting an ultimate ego-thrill and high whenever he kills. One such child in Sri Lanka, at age 12, mutilated his victims, cutting off hands of helpless civilians. He would get high first off cocaine, then plunder a village, attacking and molesting women. He had seen his own family wiped out by the monsters he now gleefully served.

Could we be witnessing something similar in the U.S.? Are we witnessing the equivalent of the soul-destroyed child-soldier of Africa or Sri Lanka here in America? Far-fetched? Absurd? Think about it. In our country, the child-killer is not being produced through a process of extreme deprivation and traumatization. Just the very opposite, in fact. In America we produce the equivalent of child-soldiers via the mass media. The cultural shift began in the 1960s when we turned our backs on the children of the world. Why should we be surprised now — a generation later — that our own children are killing each other. We have come from "Why should we care about the rest of the world?" to "Why shouldn't we kill our own classmates?"

Where have all our values gone? Selfishness and cynicism have evolved over the past quarter century into violent nihilism, a violent nihilism that is aimed at our neighbors and fellow churchgoers.

We must not turn our backs on the children and oppressed peoples of the world. That way leads only to our own self-destruction. We are, no doubt, terrified of facing the suffering that goes on among millions of people every day — suffering beyond anything we could possibly imagine. It will do us no good to bury our heads in the sand proclaiming that "those people don't really feel things the way we do." Oh, but they do. These are God's people — God's children, suffering, crying out for help, for understanding.

There is only one way we can save our own children, that is by taking responsibility for all of God's little ones, from Africa to Thailand to Guatemala. They, too, are Brothers and Sisters in Christ and deserving of our love and help. They, too, have immortal souls.

We must help to change the world so that every child has the opportunity to develop himself fully as a human being. We must love the orphans and the AIDs victims and the child-soldier with the love of Jesus Christ, for human love and compassion alone will not do the job. We need to be infused with Christ's love.

We must mobilize our own youth and admit to them our own terrible mistakes. We failed to do the job, and now this generation is faced with the awesome task — the mission — to help rebuild the world out of the rubble heap of the 20th Century — a century dominated on the one hand with technological advances, scientific discovery, and spiritual and revolutionary giants (Mother Teresa, Bishop Sheen, M.L. King, Jr.) and the frightful spectre of war (100,000,000 dead) and the threat of nuclear annihilation, coupled with rampant racism, colonialism, and racial bigotry on the other.

This generation must create a world in which no child is orphaned by war and poverty, trashed and tossed out on the scrap heap as if they were mere garbage and not a precious, unrepeatable, unique child of God, redeemed by the blood of the Lamb. A child with an immortal soul, destined for eternal life with the Trinitarian God.

This is what we must do. We must pray earnestly, trusting in God's grace, treating life like the beautiful gift it is and accepting our responsibility to help combat the Culture of Death by building a Civilization of Love, then this beloved country and world of ours will have a more blessed future.

Postscript

This book has not been written to spread despair. The opposite, in fact. For we believe — we know — that with God's help, there is much that we can do. It will require prayer, discipline, determination, and hard work. It will require much effort on our part. Is it worth all this sacrifice and hard work? Without hesitation, we can sing out an unqualified YES! For our children, our culture, are at stake. Our songs, our films, our stories, our viewing habits, our literature, must reflect our love of God and the highest of moral standards, or else the Culture of Death will reign supreme and not the Civilization of Love.

Here are some of the ways we change things for the better, followed by a list of groups and contacts you can make with folks of a like mind

You can join with others in writing letters to the Hollywood studios and TV executives expressing your opposition to specific programs and movies. Better yet, as far as television, write to the sponsors of the offending programs, then join with others in boycotting their products if your protest seems to have fallen on deaf ears. Believe me, it has worked before, numerous times, and it will work again. There is strength in numbers. Ask others to join you, or lend your support to groups who have already mounted some sort of write-in campaign, are picketing, and boycotting.

Another very effective way of showing your concern is via distribution of relevant literature. Make copies of articles addressing these issues and fax or email to others of a like mind, asking them to spread the word.

The Federal Trade Commission released a long-awaited report in 2000. The report absolutely established that major entertainment companies were deliberately marketing violent and vulgar motion pictures, recordings, and video games to young people. These moral cretins placed commercials for their products on cartoon shows and in comic books favored by children. From 1995 to 1999, even employing teenagers to promote offensive material, some 80 percent of R-rated films and 70 percent of electronic games with adult ratings were targeted specifically to children under seventeen.

As we move into 2005, several years after the FTC hearings — at which time a spokesman for the silver screen promised that "Hollywood is dedicated to rectifying past digressions" — the beat goes on. The powers-that-be in Tinseltown and in TV-Land still have their heads buried in the sand. They are still marketing a veritable tidal wave of cultural sleaze. They are still about brainwashing and contaminating our youth. They are still money-grubbers and lechers. They are still producing dirty and vulgar movies and television programs. The makers of video games are still manufacturing violence-saturated material. They are still putting out foulmouthed shock movies and grossed-out TV sitcoms. They are still making programs and motion pictures that are smutty, grotesque and obnoxiously overbearing.

We must do something to end the sleaze and dumbing-down of our culture. We must protect our children from all this garbage spewing out of Hollywood, TV, and in the violent video games such as Pokemon.

We Catholics and Christians are joining together with persons of high moral standards of all faiths in this crucial struggle against the drugs-sex-violence culture we have inherited from the Aquarian Conspiracy.

The question is: What kind of society will we bequeath to our children — one of tasteless vulgarity and scatological humor, or one that reflects the highest standards of our Judeo-Christian heritage?

You will be relieved to know that something is being done to combat those whose agenda declares, "Teen sex is okay," "parents are stupid," "violence doesn't hurt," "profanity is cool," and "morality doesn't count."

How is this being done? Our group, the Gospel of Life Disciples (GOLD), has been struggling for a long time to maintain and encourage respect for social standards. We join with others by utilizing picketing and other forms of public demonstration as time-honored and effective weapons. We distribute relevant literature. We encourage all schools (especially Catholic) to have special courses on public morality (movies, TV, books, computer games) and to welcome to their school or college persons who speak free of charge on these vital issues (Agape-GOLD has such persons). We help people write letters to the TV execs and movie studios, expressing our righteous anger at the sleaze, filth, and garbage being dumped daily on the American public.

Someone described TV as a "vast wasteland." Now is must be called "a vast toxic wasteland."

Across the board, Jew and Catholic, liberal and conservative are begging us to help stop the vulgarity and violence in all forms of entertainment. It will not stop — it will increase, unless we fellow Christians and Jews begin to care deeply enough about the alarming proliferation of such material into our lives and our homes to become actively involved.

Begin with prayer. Always with prayer. Ask our Lord and His Mother to give you the strength and courage to speak out. Remember, every time you or I buy a ticket to a violent or vulgar film, or purchase a CD laced with obscenity or even a product advertised on an offending television show, we are directly contributing to the violence, sleaze, and vulgarity that is poisoning the minds of our children and blunting the moral sensibilities of all of us.

For the sake of our children and grandchildren, and the society they will inherit and pass on to the next generations, I pray that you will join our movement and let your voice be heard. We are nonprofit, charge no joining fees or membership dues, and don't have any fund-raising activities. Any monies derived from the sale of our books, etc., is poured directly bank into our work to save our youth from Trash TV, Raunchy Radio, and Sick-O-Movies.

We can help you organize a group in your parish, school, college, or church group.

Gospel of Life Disciples (G•O•L•D)
PO Box 192
Franklin, LA 70538
     337.828.2375
     AgapeBooks2002@yahoo.com

God Bless You All.

Bibliography

Articles

Lt. Col. David Grossman, "On Killing," Executive Intelligence Review (EIR), July 2, 1999

Lyndon H. LaRouche, Jr., "Star Wars and Littleton," EIR, July 2, 1999

Linda de Hoyos, "Where Are Our Children, and What Are They Doing?," The New Federalist, March 20, 2000

Lt. Col. David Grossman, "Trained to Kill," Christianity Today, August 10, 1998

Michele Steinberg, "Report on Ritalin - The New Eugenics Tool," The New Federalist, June 12, 2000

Michele Steinberg, "Ritalin and Menticide," The New Federalist, August 21, 2000

Lyndon H. LaRouche, Jr., "The New Violence," The New Federalist, August 21, 2000

James Miller, "Rock 'N Rage," USA Today, August 18, 1999

Donald Phau, "Rock Concerts," EIR, August 21, 2000

Donald Phau, "Computer Games," EIR, March 27, 2000

Helga LaRouche, "The New Violence," video, Schiller Institute, 1999

Marjorie Mazel Hecht, numerous articles

EIR Special Report, "SATANISM, Crime Wave of the '90s," Brian Lantz, Donald Phau, Carol Hugumin, Gabriele Liebig, Steve Komm, Ed Corpus, et al.

SPECIAL THANKS TO

Brian Lantz, articles in EIR, New Federalist, and LaRouche research papers, as well as invaluable information over a 5-year period.

Also to — Michael Minnicino, Marcia Merry, Robyn Quijano, and Jeffrey Steinberg
all of whom are with the EIR research team, under the direction of Lyndon H. LaRouche, Jr., and his wonderful wife, Helga Zepp LaRouche.

Books

Oz Guiness, The Dust of Death, Intervarsity Press, Downers Grove, IL, 1973

Lt. Col. Dave Grossman, On Killing, Little Brown & Co., 1996

Vincent Bugliosi, Helter Skelter, Bantam Books, W. W. Norton, 1974.

ABOUT THE AUTHOR

Bernard Bergeron Broussard was a print journalist and columnist for 42 years. He has authored over a dozen books and scores of articles. He has been a Master Catechist, Lector, Eucharistic minister, and high school religion teacher. He was active in the civil rights movement and has been involved in movements for peace and justice for a half century. He and his wife of over 56 years, Rose Mae, organized a free health clinic for farm workers, scores of self-help co-ops, credit unions, and the nation first rent supplement program for low income families. Both husband and wife have been cited for their work by the NAACP, Catholic Church, and the Louisiana Human Relations Council.

www.ingramcontent.com/pod-product-compliance
Lightning Source LLC
Chambersburg PA
CBHW020340290526
45785CB00005B/2106